Loyalist City Streetcars

The Story of Street Railway Transit in Saint John, New Brunswick

by Fred Angus

A **Railfare** ✳ Book

Copyright 1979 by
Railfare Enterprises Limited,
Toronto, Canada. Mailing address:
Box 33, West Hill, Ontario, Canada. M1E 4R4

Book design by David R. Henderson

Published jointly by
Railfare Enterprises Limited and
The New Brunswick Museum,
277 Douglas Avenue,
Saint John, New Brunswick. E2K 1E5

ISBN 0-919130-29-1.

Contents

Above:

Various tickets of Saint John Railway Company.
New Brunswick Power Company tickets.

Opposite:

Saint John Railway Company
transfer from June 1905.

Canadian Cataloguing in Publication data:

Angus, Fred F., 1935-
    Loyalist city streetcars

ISBN 0-919130-29-1

1. Street-railroads — New Brunswick — Saint John — History. I. Title.

HE4509.S238A54   388.4'6'0971532   C79-094420-0

Foreword

CANADA'S STREET RAILWAY systems were many and varied during their history of more than a century. They ranged in size from tiny lines of only a few miles and less than half a dozen cars to the vast urban and suburban networks of Montreal, Toronto and Vancouver. While the larger systems have, understandably, been covered with varying degrees of completeness in several published works, it is only recently that the same treatment has begun to be accorded the smaller Canadian street railways. This is the first complete work to be devoted entirely to the streetcar system of Saint John, New Brunswick, and is the result of research and compilation performed intermittently over a period of fifteen years.

My interest in street railways dates back to 1947, at which time the Saint John trams were still running. During twice-yearly visits to my grandparents, Dr. and Mrs. Walter W. White of Saint John, I was an eager observer of these small red four-wheeled, double-ended streetcars, so different from the large cream and green single enders in Montreal. In 1948 our family succeeded in acquiring the body of car number 82, and it remained on my grandfather's country property for years before going to the Canadian Railway Museum in 1962.

In that year, I began to correspond with Roy Melvin of Hartford, Connecticut, whose interest in streetcars dated back to 1893. He had done considerable research on the Saint John system, and he suggested that I continue and eventually publish a history of that operation. Although I never met Mr. Melvin, he provided me with his file of correspondence on the subject as well as a valuable book of acts of the New Brunswick legislature relating to the New Brunswick Power Company and its predecessors. This was the nucleus from which the present history has come.

Unfortunately, information is often inconsistent, if not lacking entirely. This is true, especially, in the attempt to compile a rolling stock roster.

Correspondence with the former secretary of the New Brunswick Power Company revealed that records on such matters were often not kept at all; moreover, much of what was kept has not survived. Comparison of three incomplete rosters revealed that all differed from each other in some respects; photographic evidence shows that in certain cases all three were erroneous. The data on rolling stock are especially weak with regard to open cars, and few photographs have come to light showing such vehicles in identifiable poses other than some of the oldest and newest ones. The company was deficient in submitting returns to the Government on rolling stock between 1907 and 1916 with the result that annual totals of cars owned are confused and inconsistent during this important period. The roster that appears in this book, therefore, is the result of combining the available data. Even so, ambiguities have appeared and it has been necessary in these cases to make an "educated guess".

With respect to the opening and closing of lines, the available information is almost fully accurate, as these events were usually reported in the local newspapers, as well as such transportation-oriented periodicals as "The Railway and Marine World". Files of newspapers were a gold mine of information, especially for the earlier period. Like most gold mines, the nuggets were widely scattered and required much work to dig them out, although some were of great value.

Compilation of the background information would have been impossible without the assistance of many people and organizations. The New Brunswick Museum allowed me to consult its valuable files of street railway material, its newspapers and photographs. In addition, the Museum arranged for photographs to be taken of its model of car number 132. The Saint John Regional Library and the Public Archives of Canada both provided access to their newspaper files — an important source about horse cars and the early electric era, as well as minor day-to-day anecdotes which give a sense of intimacy to the account of these times. A special "thank you" must go to Lewis D. Wilson of Wilson Studio who permitted use of many unique early photographs of Saint John showing its streetcars around the turn of the century. Without these, knowledge of the details of many early cars would be scanty indeed.

Individual contributors have been many, and I would like to acknowledge the help of the following:

— The late Robert R. Brown whose article and roster in the CRHA News Report* was a foundation for further research. In addition, his photos of the Saint John trams in wartime are of great interest, and were made available by his son R. Douglas Brown.

— The late Professor Stanley Neilson who provided information about his father Matthew Neilson, General Manager of the Saint John Railway Company at the turn of the century. He provided, also, a book containing early photos, not to mention an inkwell in the shape of a streetcar that once stood on his father's desk.

— The late Lt. Col. E. M. Slader whose recollections of the army's role in quelling the 1914 riot added a new dimension to the story.

— R. Dyson Thomas of Saint John West has supplied much information and encouragement over a long period of time, in the form of news items, photos, and general comments of much interest.

* September, October, November, 1953.

Photo above:

Car No. 40 approaches the camera while a fully-loaded "sloven" heads westward. View taken on Main Street in 1906. The car is approaching the city centre on a run from Indiantown.
—Wilson Studio.

Photo below:

This photo of car 57 is the only one known of an open car of this type. The car is depicted at the old West Side car barn about 1905. As can be seen from the roof sign, it is ready to go into service on the Seaside Park line.
—Collection of Byron Wood.

— Miss Eileen C. Cushing was of great assistance in my early archival research; she, also, shared first-hand recollections of the 1914 riot.

— The late Col. C. W. Weldon MacLean recounted stories of the Saint John Railway in the days when his father, H. H. MacLean was president of the company. He kindly provided an autographed photo of Sir William Van Horne given to his father at the time of the reorganization of the company in 1894.

— George Higgins gave me a copy of a history of the Saint John transportation system which he wrote in the early 1950s.

— The late Fred Stephens of Moncton, New Brunswick provided many photos which he took himself in the 1940s. John Corby of the National Museum of Science and Technology allowed the use of additional photos from the Museum's Fred Stephens Collection.

— Peter Cox gave me a copy of the only known photo of car number 82 in service.

— William Bailey supplied an excellent builder's photograph of a Tillsonburg car.

— Harold Cox supplied data concerning the former Buffalo cars, which cleared up a puzzling question concerning the sequence of car numbers in the 1913 period.

— Omer Lavallée encouraged me to continue the work and to bring it into a condition where it could be published. He also drew the maps and offered me countless ideas and tips on how to polish up the entire project.

I have also received assistance from several relatives, but a very special thanks must go to my mother, the former Mary White of Saint John. She has patiently listened to me reading, re-reading, and discussing countless points to the extent that the term "Saint John Streetcars" must just about "drive her up the wall". In addition she has told me stories of the cars as they ran by her father's house during her girlhood, as well as such tales as how her 'Teddy Bear' was once lost by her younger sister off the open car on an early morning ride to Seaside Park. For these reasons, I would like to dedicate this book, such as it is, to my mother.

It is hoped that this history, although not as complete as I would have liked it to have been, will prove of interest both to those who knew these small red cars, and those who did not, but who may be interested in their story. Welcome aboard "Loyalist City Streetcars" and have a pleasant nostalgic ride into the trolley era of days gone by.

Fred Angus,
Montreal

1

Introduction to Saint John

THE CITY OF Saint John is the commercial metropolis and leading city of Canada's maritime province of New Brunswick. Situated on the Bay of Fundy at the mouth of the Saint John River, it possesses an excellent harbour which has made it one of the foremost winter ports in Canada. For nearly eighty years, the city was served by street cars, originally horse drawn, and, later, powered by electricity. The history of the various companies which at different times ran the street cars in Saint John is one of considerable interest, full of ambitious schemes, disappointments, frustrations, reorganizations, modernizations and innumerable anecdotes and legends. Except for the period from 1876 to 1887, the street cars ran from 1869 to 1948, and over the years the number of cars run was surprisingly large in relation to the size of the system. By the time the last trams gave way to busses most North American systems of comparable size had long since been abandoned, and the single-truck hand-braked cars were relics of a bygone era.

The coast of the Maritime provinces is of a very rugged character, and the area of Saint John is no exception. The Saint John River, in finding its way to the sea, follows an "S" shaped channel winding between rocky hills before entering the Bay of Fundy. About a mile from its mouth, it passes through a narrow gorge only a few hundred feet wide, at this point forming the world famous Reversing Falls which are, in fact, rapids, so called because at high tide the water actually flows upstream!

The central area of the city is located on a peninsula about one mile long and three-quarters of a mile wide, bounded on the west by the harbour, and on the east by Courtenay Bay, a shallow inlet from the Bay of Fundy. West of the harbour is West Saint John and Lancaster, while east of Courtenay Bay is the area known as East Saint John. Recently, the city has grown extensively towards the north and west, but for many years most of the population lived in the central area and the west side, especially on or near the peninsula where the city was founded.

The Saint John river owes its name to the fact that it was discovered by Samuel de Champlain on the festival of Saint John the Baptist, June 24th 1604, at a time when European settlement of North America was just beginning. Despite the natural advantages offered by the site, no settlement was planted. Instead, the French rulers of Acadia, as the area was then called, established their headquarters at Port Royal on the Nova Scotia side of the Bay of Fundy. In 1630, Fort Latour was built at the mouth of the Saint John River, but other than this, no perma-

Photo above:

King Street, looking down the hill towards the Market Slip about 1865. All of the buildings appearing in this picture were destroyed in the great fire of 1877.

nent community was established. For the next century or more the whole area was more in the nature of an outpost, and changed hands several times in the struggles of the Seventeenth and Eighteenth Centuries between the French and the English for control of North America. Eventually, by 1760, the English won undisputed control; in 1764, the first settlers commenced to build just north of the harbour in an area later known as Portland and, since 1889, a part of Saint John. However, settlers were few until 1783 when, at the close of the American Revolutionary War, thousands of United Empire Loyalists, refugees from the former colonies, now become the United States of America, travelled north to lands still under British rule and founded a settlement known as Parr Town, at the mouth of the Saint John River. In 1784 the Province of New Brunswick was separated from Nova Scotia, and the next year Parr Town was amalgamated with Carleton across the harbour, and incorporated as the city of Saint John, the first incorporated city in what is now Canada. Since that time Saint John has grown, until at present its population approaches 100,000 and its area spreads far beyond its original boundaries, but even today the commercial centre of the city is still on the peninsula where the Loyalists landed nearly 200 years ago.

Since the coastal areas were entirely dependent on the sea, the main means of transportation were by water; until well into the Nineteenth Century, the roads were poor and little used unless there was no alternative way to travel. As towns grew along the Saint John River, the water-borne traffic increased, and, in 1816, steamboats began a regular service between Saint John and Fredericton, the capital of New Brunswick, serving as well, intermediate villages along the river. However, in this service there was one great bottleneck. At the Reversing Falls, the entire flow of the river passes seaward through the narrow gorge at low tide, creating currents insurmountable even to steamboats, while at high tide the inward flow is almost as strong. It is only for short periods at "slack tide" each day that river vessels can pass the rapids safely and reach Saint John. Hence the southern terminal of the river steamboat service was located at Indiantown, well above the falls, and about one and three-quarter miles from the centre of Saint John. Therefore, as time went on, the need was felt for some means of regular public transportation between the city centre and the Indiantown wharves, even though, within the city itself, distances were too short to support any such public transportation. At first, stage coaches were run in conjunction with the boats. Later, as settlement spread in the 1850s, and the region between Saint John and Indiantown became the Town of Portland, rudimentary privately-owned omnibusses began running on irregular schedules on this route. As the area grew, the need for more improved service became a topic for discussion, and the result, in time, was the first street railway in the Province of New Brunswick.

Above:

The Suspension Bridge across the Reversing Falls about 1869. A similar photographic view ornamented the sides of the first horse cars of the People's Street Railway.

Below:

The paddle steamboat May Queen, built at Carleton in 1869, ran on the Saint John River until it was destroyed by fire on February 2nd 1918. The first street railway connected with such steamers at Indiantown.

—New Brunswick Museum.

—Photo by Woodburn and McClure; collection of the author.

Opposite:

Stock certificate of the People's Street Railway, issued in 1868 to Edward Willis, the editor of the Daily Morning News. Note the signature of W.K. Reynolds, also the horse car design on the corporate seal. This certificate, the only known existing share document of the pioneer company, was found during demolition of an old building in 1939.

—New Brunswick Museum.

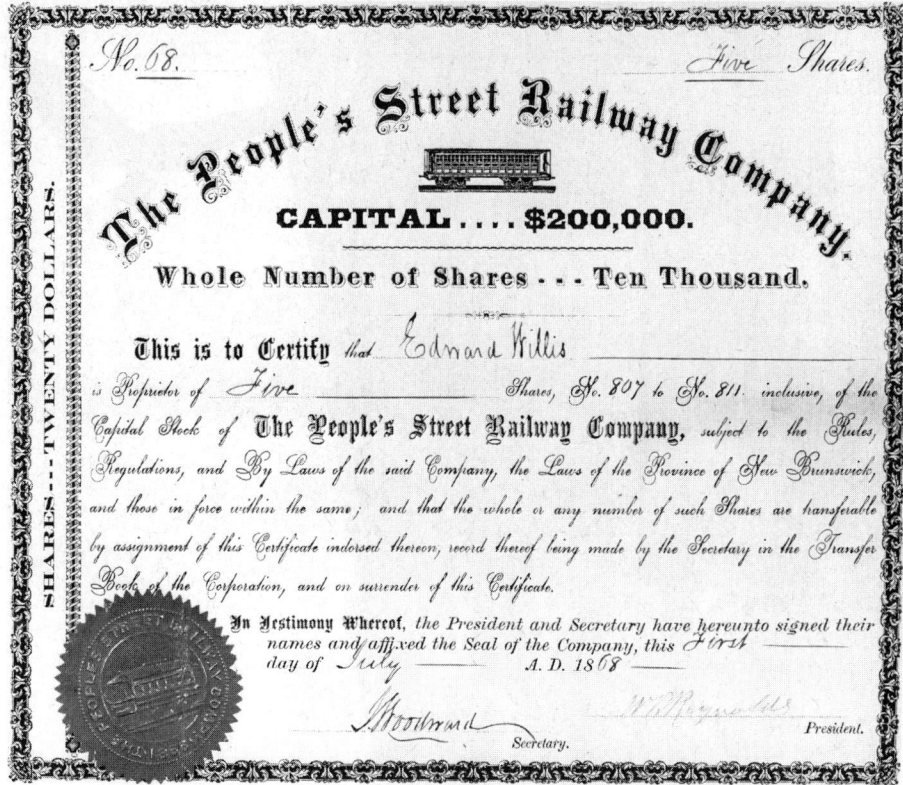

No. 68.   Five Shares.

The People's Street Railway Company

CAPITAL .... $200,000.

Whole Number of Shares - - - Ten Thousand.

This is to Certify that *Edward Willis*

is Proprietor of *Five* Shares, No. 807 to No. 811 inclusive, of the Capital Stock of The People's Street Railway Company, subject to the Rules, Regulations, and By Laws of the said Company, the Laws of the Province of New Brunswick, and those in force within the same; and that the whole or any number of such Shares are transferable by assignment of this Certificate indorsed thereon, record thereof being made by the Secretary in the Transfer Books of the Corporation, and on surrender of this Certificate.

In Testimony Whereof, the President and Secretary have hereunto signed their names and affixed the Seal of the Company, this *First* day of *July* A. D. 18*68*

Secretary.   President.

The People's Street Railway Company

THE FIRST DEFINITE steps to establish an improved regular service between Saint John and Indiantown were taken by William Kirby Reynolds, one of the many forgotten geniuses of Nineteenth Century Canada. He had already become well-known for his successful completion of a suspension bridge across the Reversing Falls, linking the East and West sides of the harbour by land. This remarkable structure, one of the engineering wonders of its day, was erected in 1853 and stood until 1916. Many years later, its inability to carry the weight of electric street cars was the reason for the division of the street railway into two physically-separate sections. Reynolds patented, in 1867, an "improved street locomotive and alarm bell", and later, in 1872, he patented a surprisingly modern-looking monorail system, and built a working model. His first proposals for a street railway came in 1864, and included a single track line from Reed's Point, along Prince

William Street to Market Square, thence by Dock, Mill, and Main streets to Indiantown. At a meeting held in the court house in Saint John it was agreed that Reynolds' scheme was of great public benefit and it was resolved to transmit to the New Brunswick Legislature, a strong recommendation in favour of the scheme. In due course, plans were drawn up and in the spring of 1866, a bill was introduced in the Legislature ". . .To incorporate 'The People's Street Railway Company' in the city and county of Saint John." The company was to be capitalized at $200,000 divided into 10,000 shares of $20. each, and provision was made to construct the street railway from Reed's Point to Indiantown within three years; this was later extended to four years. It was stipulated that the line be worked by horses, using cars on rails in the summer, and sleighs in the winter, and all privileges were to extend for forty years. The bill passed in June 1866, just before the govern-

—Public Archives of Canada, C80166.

—New Brunswick Museum.

ment fell on the issue of the proposed confederation with Canada, so ending the session. However, the act received Royal Assent on July 9th 1866, thus legally incorporating the company. At the first meeting of the new company, W.K. Reynolds was elected president, and a board of directors was set up.

Once the company had been incorporated it then became necessary to raise capital, and this was a long, slow process. By 1868 scarcely 1000 shares had been sold, but plans for the street railway slowly went ahead. Since Portland was not united to Saint John until 1889, it was necessary to secure pemission from the councils of both Saint John and Portland to allow the tracks to be laid. In June 1868, the council of Portland gave permission to the company to dig up the streets to build the line, provided that such excavations were limited to as short a time as possible. On October 28th 1868, the Common Council of Saint John consented to the company laying tracks on Prince William Street, permission having been granted already to build the Dock and Mill streets section. Thus, the entire line was covered. The specifications called for a single track in the middle of the street, constructed in such a way that no thoroughfare was to be blocked during construction, and at least 150 feet of line were completed every day, weather permitting. On Prince William Street, a paving of cobblestones was to be laid between the rails and twelve inches either side, the rest of the street being unpaved.

During the winter of 1868-69 enough additional shares were sold in New Brunswick and the New England States that a start could be made on construction, and on May 10th 1869 (the same day the last spike was driven in Utah completing the U.S. transcontinental railway) the long-awaited announcement was made that "The work on the street railway is to be resumed at once and carried through to a speedy completion". On the same day it was announced that a call would be made for a third payment of 20 percent from the stockholders, and the rails and ties were ordered. By June 28th, the rails had been delivered and on that date construction began from the Indiantown end of the line. At first work proceeded rapidly, with nineteen men clearing the roadbed, laying ties, and spiking down the rails. Progress of 500 feet per day was accomplished, but at the city end of the line — construction of which had started on July 16th — grading was more difficult, and the rails advanced much more slowly, even though 40 men were employed. By August 9th, however, the line was complete from Indiantown to

Market Square, and a start was made on the Prince William Street section. In the meantime, a carhouse and stables were built on Main Street near the Indiantown end of the line, and six cars were under construction. These vehicles were single-end one-man horsecars, of Mr. Reynolds' own design, having a front entrance at the left hand side, and no door at the rear. Usually they were pulled by two horses, but sometimes four were used. At sidings, passing was always to the left, following the rule of the road then in force in New Brunswick, right hand operation not coming until 1922. At the city end, the cars were turned by means of a small turntable, while at Indiantown, a wye was employed.

During the period of construction, considerable interest was shown by the people in the project, but some critical comment was made, as witness the two following news items, which are typical:

> "Have our citizens had time yet to admire the splendid piece of grading on the new street railway between the 'Telegraph' office and the foot of King St.? One would think they had started from the turning table with the intention of running underground to Reed's Point, and had been struck with repentance at the point referred to."
> [Daily Telegraph, August 16th 1869]

> "Mr. W.K. Reynolds denies the statement that 'miserable little T rails' are used in the construction of the street railway. The rail is known as 'centre bearing' and is considered one of the best in use for ordinary street traffic."
> [Daily Morning News, August 25th 1869]

At this time, the operators of the omnibusses, realizing that the street railway would soon put them out of business, began to run their vehicles in a very haphazard fashion, causing considerable inconvenience to the public, so it was decided to open the street railway as soon as possible. The Prince William Street section was not yet ready, nor were all the cars complete, but a trial run over the Indiantown — Market Square section was made on August 16th, and the next day, August 17th 1869, the line was informally opened. The reporter of the Daily Morning News, whose editor was a shareholder of the street railway, gave a detailed first hand account of this historic event:

> "At half past three o'clock, a neat and tastily got up car, drawn by four horses, started from the square . . . Mr. Reynolds superintended the arrangements and gave information as to the working of the railway. The cars are single (sic), passengers getting on at the front, and depositing the fare in a box prepared for the purpose, which passes down upon a trap in such a position that the driver, who also acts as conductor, can see if the amount is correct or not . . . Each car will seat something like twenty-five persons. They are got up

People's Street Railway Company.

THE above Company are desirous of Leasing the working of their Line of Railway, now in operation, (from Reed's Point, in the City of Saint John, to Indiantown, in the Parish of Portland, County of St. John,) for a term of years.

Tenders will be received at the Company's Office, Indiantown, up to WEDNESDAY, the 15th day of March, ensuing, from parties willing to lease the working of said Railway.

All Tenders to be addressed to the President and Directors "People's Street Railway Company," Indiantown, St. John, New Brunswick.

☞ All parties having accounts against the Company will please render the same to the Secretary.

W. K. REYNOLDS,

Indiantown, N. B., 21st Feb., 1871. President.

feb22   d till 15 mar

—Public Archives of Canada, L3219.

Above:

An 1871 advertisement offering to lease the operation of the People's Street Railway for five years. The line was leased in March of that year by D. Nase, who ran it until it was closed in 1876.

Below:

Prince William Street, looking south from Market Square about 1869. The three vehicles in the street appear to be horse cars. If so, this concentration of rolling stock may indicate that this is a photograph of the opening of the Prince William Street section in September 1869, and the only known photograph of the People's Street Railway. Note the awnings over the sidewalk, also the large tooth sign advertising a dentist's office. All of these buildings were completely destroyed in the 1877 fire. (See page 13.)

in good style, handsomely painted and varnished, and bearing on one side, empanneled, a photographic view of Indiantown; and on the other side one of the falls and Suspension Bridge. On this first trip the car got off the track two or three times by reason of the small stones which have not yet been entirely cleared off, as well as the horses being new to the work, but it was got on again without difficulty, and the trip from the square to Indiantown made in twelve minutes. On the return the car stopped at the company's buildings and the party were invited to inspect the premises. Here in one building we found five cars ready for the track, with the exception that two of them are not quite varnished. Six cars to go upon runners for winter use are also being built. The work is all done upon the premises under the eye of Mr. Reynolds, after whose designs the cars are built . . . The party then returned to the car, and at a few minutes before five reached the square again. Of course there was a good deal of interest excited, and it was quite amusing to see the youngsters tearing along on either side of the way to keep up with the new wonder."

The following week was spent in training the drivers and horses, and making final arrangements, and on August 24th 1869, the People's Street Railway opened for business. A car was run every twelve minutes, three cars were put on, and a few days later a fourth was added. The omnibusses were left idle, and soon shifted their field of operations elsewhere. At first the cars were crowded by curiosity seekers. Some evenings they were so overloaded that the horses could not pull them up the Indiantown hill, and

—New Brunswick Museum.

the prospects for the line looked good. But even then, there were complaints of delays, especially at passing sidings where cars were frequently held for ten minutes or more. Complaints also were made of the rails interfering with traffic, and the lack of ventilation in the cars resulted in more than one window being broken by fresh-air seeking passengers. However, these problems were considered minor, work continued, and on September 24th the Prince William Street section was opened, so completing the entire route from Reed's Point to Indiantown. Four cars were used, with two extras in rush hours, and a fare of 5¢ was charged, or 23 tickets for one dollar.

The first serious accident occurred on November 1st when a car attempted to leave a siding too soon and collided with a car going the other way. The result of this miscalculation was that one-third of the rolling stock was immobilized for two weeks. Other problems took place, but with the sudden arrival of winter on December 7th, only two sleighs were ready, so an open sleigh had to be pressed into service until the remaining four could be completed. These sleighs were much like the cars, but shorter, and travelled on runners. The sleighs were used from December to March, when the rails were again free of ice and the cars could return to service. For a week or two in March it was difficult to use either sleighs or cars, and attempts would be made to clear the track and operate cars, even resorting to the modern method of salting the streets, but frequent derailments usually ensued. In 1871, a plough was built but it was quite narrow, and some derailments still occurred.

For the next year and a half, the street railway line was operated by the company on a more or less regular basis. Occasionally, some noteworthy item would be reported in the newspapers in that unique style of prose typical of mid-Victorian journalism. The following extracts—all from the "Daily Telegraph" — are quoted verbatim:

"A number of gentlemen having occasion to go to Indiantown today at noon took the horse cars. After arriving at their destination and on enquiring what time the next car would leave they were told 'Not for an hour, the men are going to dinner'. Why could not this delay have been avoided, by having a driver in reserve for such a contingency, thus saving passengers the disagreeable necessity of walking home?"   [August 26th 1869]

—New Brunswick Museum.

Above:

An omnibus in front of the bell tower at the head of King Street about 1871. Vehicles such as this competed with the street cars until well into the Twentieth Century. The tower, constructed of wood, was a casualty of the 1877 fire.

"A narrow escape. On Monday night as No. 9 street railway car was making its last trip through Portland near Fort Howe Rock, a bullet was fired through one of the windows, passing close to the head of Mr. Kilfoyle. Its force must have been all spent as it fell within the car. No sound of firearms was heard, and no cause for the firing has been discovered."
[March 9th 1870]

"The suggestion that the broken and absent panes in the horse car windows be replaced by whole ones may not be unreasonable at the present time. The evenings are getting quite cold, and the currents of air, induced by the absence of glass in some of the cars, are not particularly good for the health of delicate persons."
[October 17th 1870]

"On Saturday night between 11 and 12 o'clock, one of our reporters observed, on crossing Market Square, a sleigh which left a white trail behind it as it wended its way. Curiosity being excited, he enquired of the driver what he was doing, and was informed that he was sprinkling salt on the rail track by order of the company for the purpose of melting the ice to allow the cars to run on wheels. Yesterday however we observed that the line had disappeared but the ice remained intact."
[February 27th 1871]

Left:

An amusing illustration which appeared in a local magazine in 1870. The compositor has combined a standard cut of an early railway car with one of a horse to depict a street railway car.

—Collection of the author.

Once the initial novelty of the street railway had worn off, it became apparent that the system was not a well-paying proposition. Maintenance was negligible and the cars deteriorated drastically. Broken steps, and missing windows were commonplace, and as the cold winds of October came there was pressure on the company at least to replace the window glass. It was alleged, too, that only one car had all its brakes working. The track had deteriorated as well, and it was found that the last 1000 feet of the Prince William Street line had been laid with ordinary bar iron, the supply of rails having given out. It was therefore a relief to passengers when winter again compelled the use of sleighs. By March 1871, debts totaled $4,000, and the financial plight of the company was so serious that it was decided to call for tenders to seek a person who would lease the undertaking for a period of years. A stormy meeting of the shareholders was held on March 17th, when several tenders were considered. One person expressed concern that the equipment was becoming badly "smashed", and he was answered that it might be well if the whole concern was "smashed" tomorrow! At length, however, an agreement was made with Mr. David Nase of Indiantown by which he would lease the entire operation for five years, starting April 1st 1871, at a rent of $750 per year. It was agreed as a condition of the lease that at least one car be run every fifteen minutes between Market Square and Indiantown, and that the route between Market Square and Reed's point be operated by at least one car per *day!* The latter section had lost the most money, and the very infrequent service was intended only to hold the franchise, despite the suggestion that small omnibusses on railway wheels, run more frequently, would show a profit. At the same time Mr. Reynolds retired as president and was succeeded by Mr. Magee. The incoming president expressed hope that the new arrangement would prove satisfactory, and that the People's Street Railway had passed its darkest days.

Under the management of Mr. Nase the line continued in regular operation and on occasions even made a small profit. Fifteen-minute service to Indiantown was maintained, and extra cars were put on to extend the service later into the evening. The most serious event of this period occurred in October 1872, when the entire line was shut down for ten days because of the epizootic of "pink eye" which threatened the horses of Eastern North America. The daily car on Prince William Street was discontinued about 1872, and on April 8th 1874 an act of the Provincial Legislature was passed ordering the company to take up the rails if it would not maintain the service. The rails were thereupon removed and sold for $1,130, the company forfeiting its right to operate on that street. About this time, five new double-ended cars were built, or rebuilt from older cars, and the

turntables were abandoned. Despite some track maintenance, the roadbed was none too good; an 1874 review reported that "Dyspeptics will find this road, like the one to Jordan, rather hard to travel, but a trip to Indiantown and back every morning before breakfast will prove of immense benefit to the digestive organs. This advice is gratis not legal".

The lease to Nase was due to expire on April 1st 1876, and as that date approached the old financial problems arose again. North America was in the midst of the very severe depression which followed the financial panic of 1873. Furthermore, numerous fires in Portland, coupled with the reduction of service on the Indiantown ferry had had a very serious effect on traffic. Faced with increasing losses, Mr. Nase curtailed service, and finally abandoned it altogether early in 1876. Tenders were again called for someone to lease the line, but this time there was no response at all. The tracks were unpopular with carters who felt that the line should be torn up, but other citizens were distressed at the possibility that "Saint John could not support even one street railway", and thought that the line could be made to pay. A meeting was held to decide what should be done, and, as expected, suggestions ranged from complete restoration of service to complete winding up of the company's affairs. At length it was decided to sell the railway's 27 horses, and this was done by auction on April 1st 1876, amid a huge crowd, prices ranging from $9 for "Old Boney" to $71 for "Billy Ferris", a total of $1,430 being realized. Since the rolling stock did not eat, it was decided to keep it for the time being. An inventory was taken and revealed five new double door cars in good condition, one old car in poor condition still lettered "Reed's Point and Indiantown", and five sleighs. Unfortunately, the car numbers were not reported, and, apart from the fact that car No. 9 was in service in March 1870, nothing is known of the numbering system used. During the course of the meeting a shareholder suggested that a dividend distribution might be made, and he was answered that since this was the (U.S.) centennial year, any dividends should be deferred until the next centennial! In summing up, the president declared the whole situation to be "a pretty sick affair".

Once the cars had really stopped, the residents of Portland and Indiantown realized the benefits they had given. Some offers were made to operate the route, but it was the old story of "too little, too late".

On June 21st 1876, the company held its annual meeting, and it was decided to press the claim against Mr. Nase for $2,791.62 for depreciation and arrears on rent. Depreciation was high because for the preceding three years the line had been allowed to run down with little being

spent for upkeep. A debate then ensued on what to do with the street railway, and it was finally resolved to wind up the affairs of the company before it ate up all the assets, as it had "eaten up the horses". The directors were authorized to dispose of all property including cars, rails, buildings and leases, but to retain the charter in case conditions changed in the future, a wise decision as it turned out. The rails were sold to Harris & Company, the car builders, who began to lift them from the streets on July 18th. Thus, by the end of the summer of 1876, the line of the People's Street Railway was no more.

There is no record of what happened to the cars; at least one body is known to have been used as a shed in Saint John in 1877, but all soon disappeared. The omnibusses returned to the route, and things were much as they had been before 1869. The charter, however, still had thirty years to run, so there was still talk of someday rebuilding the line. One or two proposals were made to reorganize with new capital as soon as the depression ended, but all these plans were, temporarily at least, forgotten, following the catastrophic events of June 20th 1877.

In the afternoon of that day, a fire began near the corner of Union and Smyth Streets and, fanned by a high wind, the flames soon spread widely among the wooden buildings which then comprised most of the city. Within the short space of nine hours, almost the entire central portion of Saint John, south of King Street from water to water, had been completely destroyed. Among the many sufferers that day was the People's Street Railway Company, which lost all of its records, books and accounts.

A small anecdote of this day of disaster tells of an exhausted young woman who, fleeing from the flames, sought refuge in an abandoned horse car body, and there gave birth to a baby while the fire was at its height. Both mother and child survived, but the car was almost certainly burned within hours. This is the last mention of any of the old rolling stock, most of which either perished in the fire or was otherwise soon destroyed.

In the general disaster and subsequent rebuilding of the burned district, which amounted to almost half of the city, the plans for a revived street railway were forgotten. Thus for another decade Saint John was without street cars, and the entire enterprise lay dormant.

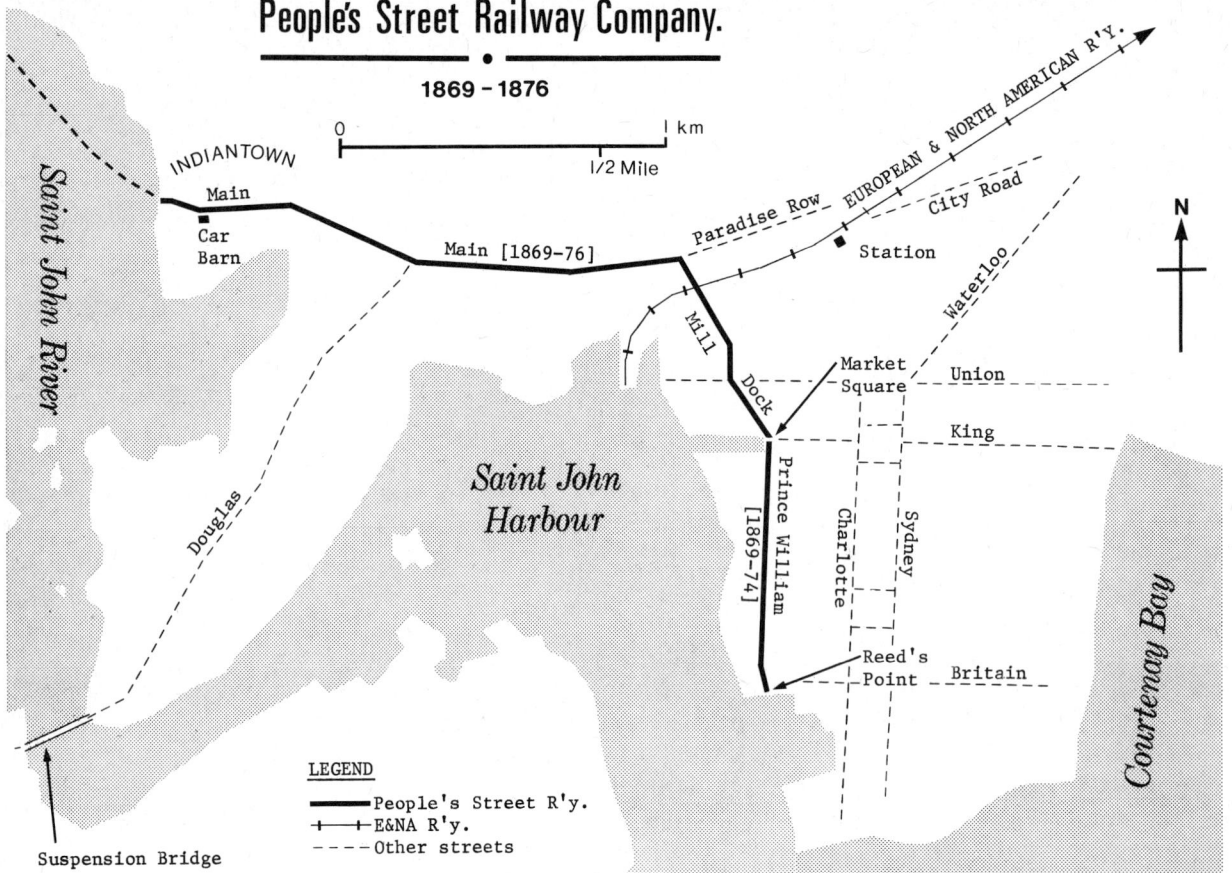

People's Street Railway Company.

●

1869 – 1876

0 _____ 1 km

1/2 Mile

INDIANTOWN

Main

Car Barn

Main [1869–76]

Saint John River

Paradise Row

EUROPEAN & NORTH AMERICAN R'Y.

City Road

Station

Waterloo

Mill

Dock

Market Square

Union

King

Saint John Harbour

Prince William [1869–74]

Charlotte

Sydney

Reed's Point

Britain

Courtenay Bay

N

Douglas

Suspension Bridge

LEGEND
———— People's Street R'y.
—+—+— E&NA R'y.
– – – Other streets

3 Saint John
City Railway Company

$\mathcal{D}$URING THE 1880s street railways spread to more and more North American cities, and became almost a necessity of life. In Saint John the opinion was often expressed that it was unfortunate that the street railway had come to such an ignominious end, and that, in the light of increasing popularity of public transportation elsewhere, the time might soon be ripe for giving the enterprise a second chance. The People's Street Railway Company still existed, but most of the records were destroyed, and the stock was considered so nearly worthless that few shareholders had even bothered to request new stock certificates to replace those destroyed in the fire. The most important obstacle barring any plan to rebuild the railway was, of course, the raising of capital. For some years after the fire, most available capital was used in rebuilding the city and, furthermore, since so many investors had lost heavily in the collapse of the PSR, the feeling of "once bitten, twice shy" was very strong. However, by the mid 1880s, the scars of 1877 were healed; in 1886, an offer to finance a street railway came from a syndicate of New York capitalists, headed by J.F. Zebley, which was then in the process of reorganizing the Halifax Street Railway. On August 5th 1886, an agreement was reached with the PSR shareholders by which the entire rights, privileges and franchises of the People's Street Railway were leased to James Platt, the agent of the syndicate.

A charter was obtained by the syndicate in New York in September 1886, incorporating "The Saint John City Railway Company", which was capitalized at $300,000. On April 5th 1887, the Legislature of New Brunswick modified the

charter of the People's Street Railway Company, recognized the reorganization of the company and its lease to the New York syndicate. The New York company was reincorporated in New Brunswick on the same date, enabling it to take over all of the assets and franchises of the People's Street Railway Company.

The basic conditions of the new agreement were much the same as those of 1866, but some changes were made. The restriction imposed in 1874 against operating cars on Prince William Street was removed and, in view of the promise that electricity showed for the future, permission was granted to use any form of motive power, except that steam could be used only if approved by the City Council. Plans included not only the reconstruction of the entire line from Indiantown to Reed's Point, but an extension was to be built from the latter location up St. James Street to Carmarthen Street. A new line was to branch off the main line near the railway station, and run along Paradise Row; Wall, Winter and Stanley streets; and City Road to Haymarket Square. It was stipulated in the Act that work must begin no later than the spring of 1887, and that the line from Indiantown to Market Square as well as the branch to Haymarket Square must be completed within one year or the charter would be void.

By the time that the company was incorporated in New Brunswick, considerable capital had been raised, largely in New York, and construction work had actually begun. As early as February 7th, B.W. Ellis had been appointed consulting engineer, and Harris & Company, the well known car builders of Saint John, had been given the contract to roll the rails. These rails were conventional horse car "step" rails, spiked to wooden stringers. Since the site of the old car barn had been sold, a two-acre lot on the south side of Main Street, closer to the city, was purchased, and a car barn and stable erected thereon. This building survived well into the electric car era, not being disposed of until 1925. Over one hundred horses were stabled in a large building adjacent to the carbarn.

Photo opposite page:

A horse car, travelling north on Prince William Street towards Market Square, passes a "sloven" outside the Bank of New Brunswick (now Bank of Nova Scotia) on a sunny morning about 1890. Most of the buildings in the picture were built within two years of the fire of 1877, and many still stand today.

—New Brunswick Museum.

Construction of the track began in the spring of 1887, and proceeded rapidly with little interruption. By July 30th, the main line was complete and the stables were nearly ready. On September 21st, the Common Council gave permission to the company to construct the branch line from Reed's Point via St. James Street to Carmarthen Street, and work began at once. The same evening, the schooner *Mabel Purdy* docked in port bringing the first two streetcars, and the next morning two more cars arrived on the schooner *Thresher*. These cars were constructed by M. Feigel Car Company, New Utrecht, New York, (now a part of Brooklyn) and were described as being finely built and seated, and twenty feet long over all. Two snow ploughs were ordered from Harris & Company for delivery in time for winter. The company decided not to begin service until the St. James Street extension was complete and more cars were available; however, some trips were made without passengers for the purpose of training drivers and horses, as well as to iron out operating difficulties.

Finally, the official opening was set for October 17th. On the morning of the sixteenth, the schooner *Avis* brought four more street cars, bringing to eight the number ready for service on the opening day. Two more cars, delivered soon after the opening, completed the ten cars ordered from Feigel.

—Public Archives of Canada, L5835.

St. John City Railway Co'y,
October 15th, 1887.

NOTICE.

On AND AFTER TUESDAY, OCT. 18th, Cars will run between INDIANTOWN LANDING, Portland, and Cor. St. James and CARMARTHEN Streets, St. John, as follows:

Leaving Indiantown at 6.10, 6.30 a. m., and every 15 minutes until 8.00 a. m.; then every 10 minutes until 8.00 p. m.; after that every 15 minutes until 10.30 p. m.

Returning from Cor. St. James and Carmarthen Streets, 6.35, 6.55 a. m., and every 15 minutes until 8.25; then every 10 minutes until 8.25 p. m.; after that every 15 minutes until 10.55 p. m.

The Last Car will leave Market Square at 11.02 p. m.

The Fare will be FIVE CENTS for one continuous ride.
Children under four years will be allowed to ride free. If occupying seats they will be charged full fare.
Change to the amount of $2.00 will be furnished by the driver, who will return the full amount.
Under no circumstances will the driver be allowed to receive or deposit a fare.

B. W. ELLIS, JR.,
Superintendent.

"READY FOR THE PEOPLE" proclaimed the Daily Telegraph when describing the events of the formal opening. The ceremonies were scheduled to get under way at 3:00 PM, but due to the large crowds present, as well as the late arrival of some of the invited guests who were to board the cars at the depot, it was 3:45 before the first car reached Market Square. Soon, all eight cars were lined up at the Square,

". . . . .where they presented a sight well worth looking at. Fresh from the shop, their polished surfaces were perfect reflectors, and the swiftness and quietness with which they moved over the road made everyone wish to get aboard and enjoy a ride."

In a few minutes the first car, in charge of conductor Swan, started off and led the procession as all eight cars then covered the entire line, including the section to Carmarthen Street which had only been completed a few days previously. Only one incident slightly marred the proceedings. On Mill Street,

". . . . .a drunken Haligonian had mounted the driver's steps, and so interfered with him while going down the hill that he could not apply the brakes in proper time, the result being that the horses became somewhat excited and swerving to one side broke the pole. The car had gained such an impetus that it ran against one of the horses and injured it somewhat. To show how slight an impediment such an accident is to traffic it can be said that the car was moved to one side and the track clear in almost less time than it takes to write it, and those following whirled swiftly by the scene and around the foot of Main Street into Paradise Row."

As soon as the cars arrived at the depot, having also covered the line to Haymarket Square and back, a gala reception was held to celebrate the event. The host "had provided everything which is supposed to make men genial and social" and as a result many toasts were drunk, starting with Queen Victoria and President Cleveland of the United States, and there was much singing and speechmaking. At length a toast was proposed to Messrs. Zebley and Ellis, who were called the "heroes of cars"*. The festivities continued until 7:00 PM, and next day the first regular service was begun by the Saint John City Railway.

The almost universal celebration over the street railway opening soon turned to shocked surprise when it was realized that the company actually intended to run the cars on Sunday! In the 1880s many street railways ran only six days a week, and the thought of Sunday street car service was looked upon in many quarters as a sin and a profanation of the Sabbath. "SHALL THEY RUN SUNDAY?" was the question

Left:
Newspaper notice announcing the opening of the St. John City Railway in 1887. Note that the Haymarket Square line is not yet operating.

A horse car passing through Market Square about 1887. Note the many ships in the background.
—New Brunswick Museum.

asked, and on Friday, October 21st a petition, signed by twenty-two church ministers, was presented to Mr. Zebley. Among other objections the clergy feared that Sunday street cars would lead to "the getting up of excursions and other attractions" by which "a very deep injury would be done to the religious interests of the people". The possibility that some people might use the street cars to go to church seems to have been lost on these gentlemen; besides, one was free to avoid travel by street car on Sunday if one did not want to. The answer of Mr. Zebley was short and to the point: "I shall run the cars on Sunday." Accordingly, on October 23rd, the first Sunday car ran in Saint John, and although several sermons were preached on 'the desecration of the Sabbath,' the tempest-in-a-teapot soon died out. Sunday service continued as long as the street cars ran, without causing any significant injury to the religious.

Very soon it became fashionable to "go to Indiantown for a drive" as people took advantage of the novelty of the cars. It had been almost twelve years since street cars had run, and the new ones were such an improvement over the old cars of 1869 - 1876 that riding them was a completely new experience. Many persons had never travelled on a street car before, and the cars became the main topic of conversation for several weeks. Street car stories began to circulate, such as that of the man who accidently dropped a fifty-cent piece into the fare box and, on finding that he could not get change, proceeded to stay on the car and ride back and forth ten times to get his money's worth. Another story tells of a man who wanted to get off,

* a word play on "The Heroes of Kars" in the Crimean War.

pulled the hand strap instead of the bell cord, and was carried half a mile too far before he realized his mistake.

During the winter of 1887-88, service was provided with sleighs as had been done before, but on March 8th an attempt was made to run the cars. This was temporarily frustrated by more snow, probably an offshoot of the famous "blizzard of '88," but by April the cars were running again. In April the whole line was ballasted, making a smoother, safer ride than on the track as originally laid. About this time a proposal was made for a subway to run under the harbour to connect the east and west sides. The horse cars would have been extended to run through this tunnel, which would thus have been the first underground city railway in Canada. But the plan came to nothing, as it was far ahead of its time and would have been much too costly; in fact no street car would run on the west side for another fifteen years.

However, extensions to the horse car line were soon to be built; first a double track was laid on Main street in the vicinity of the car barn, and when this was completed work began on building the Brussels Street line on June 18th, 1888. This new line was planned to extend from the terminus of the existing branch line at Haymarket Square, double back along Brussels Street (now Prince Edward Street), then via Union and Charlotte streets to the head of King Street. From this point, it was hoped to run down King Street, the main shopping street of Saint John, to join the old line at Market Square. The roadbed was completed to the corner of King and Charlotte Streets by July 11th, the rails were soon laid, and, unlike the original main line, were fully ballasted from the start. Service began on August 22nd, passengers transferring as before at the corner of Main Street and Paradise Row. Four cars gave a fifteen-minute

Saint John City Railway horse car standing in front of a typical wooden Saint John house. Car 5 is one of the original Feigel-built cars of 1887.

—Wilson Studio.

—New Brunswick Museum.

TRAINS LEAVE INDIANTOWN FOR ST. JOHN.			TRAINS LEAVE MARKET SQUARE FOR CARMARTHEN ST.			TRAINS LEAVE MARKET SQUARE FOR INDIANTOWN.			TRAINS LEAVE CARMARTHEN ST. FOR INDIANTOWN.			TRAINS LEAVE FOOT OF PORTLAND FOR HAYMARKET SQ.		TRAINS LEAVE HAYMARKET SQUARE.	
A.M.	A.M.	P.M.	A.M.	P.M.	P.M.	A.M.	P.M.	P.M.	A.M.	P.M.	P.M.	A.M.	P.M.	A.M.	P.M.
5.57	11.39	4.39	6.13	12.07	5.13	6.34	12.04	*5.10	6.27	12.03	*5.15	6.27	4.39	6.39	4.45
6.09	11.51	*4.45	6.25	12.19	5.19	6.46	12.10	5.16	6.39	12.09	5.21	6.57	4.57	7.15	4.57
6.27	P.M.	4.51	6.43	12.31	5.25	7.04	12.16	*5.22	6.57	12.21	5.27	7.27	5.15	7.39	5.15
*6.45	12.03	4.57	7.01	12.43	5.31	*7.22	12.28	5.28	*7.15	12.33	*5.33	7.57	5.27	8.09	5.27
7.03	*12.15	*5.03	7.19	12.55	5.37	7.40	12.40	5.34	7.33	*12.45	5.39	8.09	5.45	8.27	5.45
*7.15	12.27	5.09	7.31	1.01	5.43	7.52	*12.52	*5.40	7.45	12.57	*5.45	8.27	5.57	8.39	5.57
7.27	12.39	*5.15	7.43	1.07	5.49	*8.04	1.04	5.46	*7.57	1.09	5.51	8.39	6.09	8.57	6.15
7.39	*12.45	5.21	7.55	1.13	5.55	8.16	1.16	*5.52	8.09	*1.15	*5.57	8.57	6.27	9.12	6.27
7.51	12.51	5.27	8.07	1.19	6.07	8.28	*1.22	5.58	8.21	1.21	6.03	9.12	6.39	9.27	6.45
*7.57	12.57	*5.33	8.13	1.31	6.19	*8.34	1.28	*6.04	*8.27	1.27	6.09	9.27	6.57	9.45	6.57
8.03	1.03	5.39	8.19	1.43	6.31	8.40	1.34	6.10	8.33	*1.33	6.21	9.39	7.15	9.57	7.15
......	*1.15	5.51	......	1.55	6.43	8.46	*1.40	6.16	8.39	*1.45	6.33	9.57	7.27	10.15	7.27
8.09	1.27	6.03	8.25	2.07	6.55	*8.52	*1.52	6.28	*8 45	*1.57	*6.45	10.27	7.39	10.45	7.45
*8.15	1.39	*6.15	8.31	2.19	7.07	8.58	*2.04	6.40	8.51	2.09	6.57	10.57	7.57	11.15	7.57
8.21	1.51	*6.27	8.37	2.25	7.19	9.04	2.16	*6.52	8.57	2.21	•7.09	11.27	8.09	11.45	8.15
8.27	2.03	6.39	8.43	2.31	7.31	9.10	2.28	7 04	9.03	*2.33	7.21	11.57	8.27	P.M.	8.27
8.33	2.09	6.51	8.49	2.37	7.37	9.16	*2.40	7.16	9.09	2.39	7.33	P.M.	8.39	12.15	8.45
8.39	*2.15	*7.03	8.55	2.43	7.43	*9.22	2.46	7.28	*9.15	*2.45	*7.45	12.27	8.57	12.39	8.57
*8.45	2.21	*7.15	9.01	2.49	7.49	9.28	*2.52	7.40	9.21	2.51	7.51	12.39	9.27	12.57	9.15
8.51	2.27	7.21	9.07	2.55	7.55	*9.34	2.58	*7.52	*9.27	*2.57	*7.57	12.57	9.57	1.12	9.45
8.57	*2.33	*7.27	9.13	3.01	8.01	9.40	*3.04	7.58	9.33	3.03	8.03	1.12	10.27	1.27	10.15
9.03	2.39	7.33	9.19	3.07	8.13	9.46	3.10	*8.04	9 39	3 09	8.09	1.27	......	1.45	10.39
9.09	*2.45	7.39	9.25	3.13	8.19	*9.52	3.16	8.10	*9 45	3.15	*8.15	1.45	......	1.57	
*9.15	2.51	*7.45	9.31	3.19	8.31	9.58	3.22	8.16	9.51	3.21	8.27	1.57	......	2.15	
9.21	2.57	*7.57	9.37	3.25	8.43	10.04	3.28	*8.22	9.57	3.27	8.33	2.09	......	2.27	
*9.27	3.03	8.03	9.43	3.31	8.55	10.10	3.34	8.34	10.03	3.33	*8.45	2.27	......	2.45	
9.33	3.09	*8.15	9.49	3.37	9.07	10.16	3.40	8.40	10.09	3.39	8.57	2.45	......	2.57	
9.39	*3.15	*8.27	9.55	3.43	9.19	*10.22	3.46	*8.52	*10.15	*3.45	9.09	2.57	......	3.15	

—From the *Dominion Illustrated;* courtesy New Brunswick Museum.

SUMMER

TIME TABLE

OF THE

SAINT JOHN

City Railway Co.

TRAINS ARE RUN ON TIME AS
FURNISHED BY

Page,
Smalley &
Ferguson,
JEWELLERS,
43 King Street,
ST. JOHN, N. B.

Above:

In 1892, a horse car passes the New Victoria Hotel on Prince William Street, while an elegant four-wheeled carriage waits outside.

Timetable left and upper right:

Timetable issued by the Saint John City Railway Company in the summer of 1888. Note that the horse cars are referred to as "trains".

service on the new line, necessitating the purchase of new cars in 1888, which brought the total number of cars to fourteen. They ran on seven miles of track, the total extent of horse car operation. One more car appears to have been acquired in 1889 but no new track was laid until 1894, after electrification. Although the terminus of the extended line was only two blocks up King Street from Market Square, it was decided not to attempt to close the gap and create a loop line. This was partly due to financial reasons, but, most likely recognized as well that the very steep grade on King Street was beyond the capabilities of horse cars to negotiate with safety. Thus a passenger wishing to travel by street car two blocks up the hill would have to go two miles over a roundabout route. In the electric car days, the King Street line was built and became the busiest line in the city.

Once the cars were running, things went smoothly. A ten-minute headway was provided on the Indiantown-Carmarthen Street line, with fifteen-minute service on the Haymarket Square and Brussels Street branch. On hills, extra horses were hitched on to pull the car up and maintain scheduled speed. Extra cars were run in the baseball season, and also in connection with the excursion steamers on the river. In 1888, new uniforms were provided for the crews featuring double-breasted coats, silver buttons, hats "like those of Pullman conductors" and badges lettered either "Driver" or "Conductor". Service was maintained on such a regular basis that the company actually issued a public timetable giving the times that cars passed principal points. In the winter, sleighs, nine open and six closed, were used, and straw was placed on the floor to keep passengers' feet warm, but the track was kept open as long as possible, with the new shear ploughs and diggers using a six-horse hitch. Within a short time, the street railway had become more of a necessity than a luxury and the people of Saint John were proud of the new horse car system which was considered to be, for its size, one of the best-run in Canada.

4 | The Start of
Electrification

$\mathcal{T}$HE DECADE OF the Nineties ushered in a new era, and it did not take much imagination to predict that this would be the decade in which electricity would establish itself as the dominant force in urban public transit. The practicability of electric traction had now been proved beyond a doubt, and the age of the trolley was dawning.

In Canada, by 1890, some electric lines had been established for as long as five years, and very soon all major Canadian cities would electrify their street railway systems. The Saint John City Railway Company had anticipated possible future use of electric traction as early as 1887, and received specific legislative permission in 1890 to electrify its lines. In the same year, two companies, The New Brunswick Electric Company, and the Eastern Electric Company, were chartered for the purpose of supplying electric light and power to Saint John. These companies were allied with the management of the street railway, but were not directly connected with it until 1892. On January 18th of that year, a new company, The Consolidated Electric Company, was incorporated, acquiring all the assets of both power companies as well as the Saint John City Railway Company.

Immediately, The Consolidated Electric Company announced plans to electrify and extend the street railway system in Saint John, including constructing the King Street route, and sought permission in the form of an act of the Provincial Legislature. Passage of this act was not accomplished without difficulty, the chief objection being clauses permitting the company to clear snow from the streets in order to allow cars to operate in winter, thereby interfering with privately-owned sleighs. Another bone of contention was the granting to the company of exclusive privileges for forty years. Notwithstanding these objections, and even threats by some city councillors to "tear up the tracks" of the "upstart" street railway, the act was passed on April 7th 1892, giving the company full privileges to operate an electric street railway in Saint John.

The remainder of 1892 saw plans for electrification proceed, and necessary money raised. Six electrified horse cars were bought from the West End Street Railway of Boston, Massachusetts, and poles and trolley wire erected. No attempt was made to relay the track; instead, the flat horsecar rails were hastily bonded. Although a copper ground wire was laid between the rails and connected to them at intervals, in places the only connection was made by a spike tightly driven in between the rail ends. As the first quarter of 1893 drew to a close, the start of electric traction was anticipated more and more eagerly. "The electric surface railway is soon to be a reality, and the cry of the motorman will be heard in the land" announced papers that spring, as the conversion neared completion. Yet there were still many skeptics. Dire predictions were made of the serious effects of the high speeds (up to 25 miles an hour!), and "nerve racking" noise, as well as the danger of electrocution from falling wires. One elderly citizen deplored the possibility of "seeing a car with a fishing pole on top tearing at breakneck speed down King St., leaving the tracks, and perhaps going over the wharf at Market Slip and drowning all on board". This last fear was voiced all through the days of the electric cars, and although cars ran away on at least two hills in the early days, there is no recorded instance of a serious runaway street car on King Street hill in all of the 54 years of electric operation. This is perhaps not so much a testimony to the reliability of hand brakes as it was to pure good luck. Nevertheless, the many hills negotiated by the cars always made operation very difficult, especially in winter. The problem was never really solved, and was one of the causes of later complaints of unsatisfactory service.

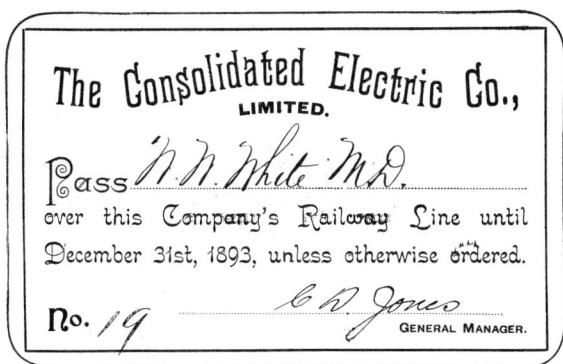

The Consolidated Electric Co.,
LIMITED.

Pass *W. W. White M.D.*
over this Company's Railway Line until
December 31st, 1893, unless otherwise ordered.

No. *19*
                                    C. D. Jones
                                    GENERAL MANAGER.

By Good Friday, March 31st 1893, work had progressed to the point where a test run could be made, and on that day, just as churchgoers were leaving the afternoon Good Friday services, the first electric street car ran in Saint John. On April 1st, the Daily Telegraph announced:

"Yesterday the first electric car made its appearance on the streets of St. John. It did not make a trip over the whole route, but confined itself to the few hundred yards of space between a little above the car sheds and towards the foot of Indiantown. The car was brought out from the car sheds at about 3 o'clock, in charge of electrician Bliss, and was found to work very satisfactorily. A large crowd nearly blockaded the street while the car was on the route. A car will be run over the entire road in a few days."

On the evening of April 3rd, the second test run was made, and the company ran a special car (horse car of course) from the city to carry spectators who wished to see this test. Weather conditions could not have been worse, as the run was carried out in the midst of snow, sleet, and freezing rain which coated both rails and trolley wire, and made operation most difficult. Nevertheless, the test was "not altogether disappointing" and since the management evidently felt that if the cars could cope with that kind of weather they could cope with anything, public service was started on April 12th 1893. One car was run, concurrently with horse cars, between Indiantown and Market Square, and as the "brilliantly lighted" car "whizzed" by the horse cars at passing sidings it was obvious that the days of the horse cars were numbered. Within a week the entire Indiantown - Market Square service was provided by five electric cars taking twelve minutes to make the run, and the work of electrifying the remaining lines was speedily pushed to completion. Early in May, the last horse car made its final run, and on July 19th, the last fourteen of the street railway horses were sold at auction for about $25 per horse.

The cars acquired from Boston were former horsecars with sixteen-foot bodies, equipped with Bemis trucks and 15 horsepower motors. As electrification proceeded, cars with twelve-foot bodies made their appearance, and it is probable that these were some of the old Saint John horse cars equipped with electric motors. However, during the reorganization proceedings in 1894, a Massachusetts lawyer claimed that his client had leased the cars to the Consolidated Electric Company for $55,000 for five years. This was considered to be much too high a price in view of the condition and semi-obsolescence of these vehicles.

Cartoon depicting street car travel, published in the Daily Telegraph. *on December 28th 1894.*
— New Brunswick Museum.

Obliging Irishman: "I'll be wan av two gintlemin to give the leddy a sate."
—Scribner's Magazine.

All the electric cars of the Company were electrified horse cars either from Boston or Saint John; all had wooden trolley poles and were single-ended, being turned on wyes at each end of the line. A new 133 horsepower generator was installed; this unit was similar to that previously used for electric lighting but was much larger, weighing 8½ tons. It was the largest electric machine then in use in the Maritime provinces. The power house was situated at the South-West corner of Dock and Union Streets, and still stands today, although much enlarged, having served throughout the entire fifty-five year period of electric car operation.

The Consolidated Electric Company had planned to construct a new track on King St. and so complete the loop line to provide more convenient service. However, by the time that all the expenses of the conversion to electricity had been met, the company was in a shaky financial situation. Moreover it soon became obvious that the horse car rails were unsuitable for carrying the faster and heavier electric cars, and in fact the cars themselves, being horse cars of relatively light construction, suffered from the higher speeds and occasional derailments. No really serious mishaps took place, although annoying little misfortunes cropped up with unpleasant frequency. Car number 20 seemed to be the most jinxed; on June 30th 1893, a lad named Brown entered the car barn, started this car, and drove it out at full speed into the street where it promptly derailed, with some damage. The company took no action against the unfortunate Brown when his father promised to "look after him". Later, on August 14th, the motorman of car 20 was suspended for running into and demolishing an express wagon on Prince William Street, and as if this was not enough, the following May 24th, some youngsters on Main Street, celebrating Queen Victoria's Birthday, threw a package of firecrackers under the same car and set fire to the canvas hung under the motors to protect them from mud. But other cars had their troubles too. Probably due to the unfamiliarity of the public with the new cars, there were numerous collisions with wagons and carriages, but no one was seriously hurt. The closest approach to a fatal accident happened on June 2nd 1893 when conductor Shaw, noticing that his car was not running well, looked out from the back platform and was hit on the head by a 4½-pound trolley wheel which fell from the end of the pole and "about used Shaw up", inflicting painful, but as it proved, not serious injuries. The wooden trolley poles gave trouble, and several times cars were immobilized by broken poles.

Opposite, upper photo:

Electric car No. 21 on Charlotte Street at the head of King in 1894. This appears to be one of the 1887 Saint John horse cars converted to electric operation in 1893. Note the wooden trolley pole.
— New Brunswick Museum.

In spite of the shortage of money, improvements were made. As the winter approached, experimental electric heaters were installed in car No. 17; these proved so successful that they were soon put in all cars. Following a serious snowstorm on December 9th, in which each car used a pailful of sand on each trip, and service was very late, a flanger car was quickly equipped and cleared the snow satisfactorily. But the street railway did not have a sweeper, and in the very heavy snowstorm of January 15th 1894, so much snow fell that the electric cars were completely blocked and the tracks had to be dug out by hand, a process which took nearly a week. Service was greatly curtailed, and it was not until January 21st that cars again ran through to Indiantown. The only other major interruption to service was caused by an accident to the powerhouse boiler in February 1894, which resulted in all power being cut off.

Despite these problems, the electric railway passed through its first winter so well that the ultimate success of electric traction in the New Brunswick climate was well assured. By 1894, however, the company was in very serious financial difficulties. Certainly, further extension was out of the question, even though the proposed King Street route would bring in much needed additional revenue. Maintenance on the track and equipment was minimal, and deterioration of the system became evident. The syndicate's other Maritime interest, the Halifax Street Railway, had fared even worse, and had not even been electrified. As the winter progressed, things went from bad to worse, and in March it was announced that the Consolidated Electric Company was bankrupt, and that the entire street railway and lighting plant of Saint John would be sold at public auction on Saturday, April 7th 1894.

5

Complete Rebuilding

IN THE HISTORY of the Saint John street car system, 1894 probably stands out as the most important year of all. It was in this year that the entire system was completely reorganized, rebuilt, and placed on a sound footing. In this year also, it took on the character which it retained for the remainder of its existence.

As April 7th and the auction sale drew nearer, there was very much speculation as to who, if anyone, would purchase the street railway. Would it be rescued, or would it, after all the effort put into it, suffer the fate of the old People's Street Railway? When the sale was over, it was announced that the system had been sold for $92,000, the successful bidder being E.C. Jones, representing a syndicate of capitalists from both Montreal and Saint John. The new syndicate included such notables as Sir William Van Horne, James Ross, Richard B. Angus and Sir Thomas Shaughnessy of Montreal; and Hugh H. McLean and H.P. Timmerman of Saint John. Most of these gentlemen were prominent in the Canadian Pacific Railway, and this is not surprising since the CPR whose trains had first reached Saint John in 1889 via the "Short Line" through Maine, was now actively engaged in improving the terminal and port facilities to make Saint John the eastern ocean terminal of its transcontinental system, and a future winter port of Canada. However, it is due largely to the initiative of H.H. McLean that the Montreal capitalists were made aware of the opportunity presented by the sale to acquire the street railway at a bargain price.

Within a few days, Van Horne and Ross were making plans for the improvement of their newly-acquired electric railway. It was obvious that major renovations would be needed, and within a week the public was informed that the entire system would be rebuilt at a cost of $300,000. On April 16th, the trustees of the

Consolidated Electric Company transferred all the assets of that company to the new syndicate, and on April 21st, 1894, an act of the New Brunswick Legislature incorporated The Saint John Railway Company. The processes of law moved with unbelievable speed, and within two weeks of the sale the complicated financial tangle of the various predecessor companies had been straightened out. The new company had a solid financial base, and a new forty-year franchise to operate street cars in Saint John with all the rights granted to the earlier companies.

Being familiar with the energy and enterprise of the heads of the new company, the people of Saint John counted on great things being done for the street railway; but the plans submitted to city council on April 24th must have surprised even the most hopeful. These plans called for the tearing up of all the old track, and the construction of an entirely new system, consisting of 11½ miles of track, much more extensive than the previous one. Three routes would be operated, the first, being by far the largest, would be served by at least eight cars running at five-minute intervals. This route would start at Indiantown and proceed to Market Square, at which point alternate cars would loop through the streets of the South end in different directions. One car would go up King Street hill,

Opposite, upper:

Market Square in 1906. Cars Nos. 31 and 40 have just passed, and a passenger is boarding the latter car for Main Street and Indiantown.

—Wilson Studio.

Opposite, lower:

Open car No. 46 in Market Square at 12:15 PM, October 7th 1901. This car, built in Montreal in 1898, is similar to the Montreal open cars of 1898 except that it is built for left-hand operation. However, the controller position is not reversed. This is an enlargement of a portion of a photograph taken by Canadian Pacific Railway photographer Joseph W. Heckman to show his company's headquarters building in Saint John.

—Canadian Pacific Corporate Archives.

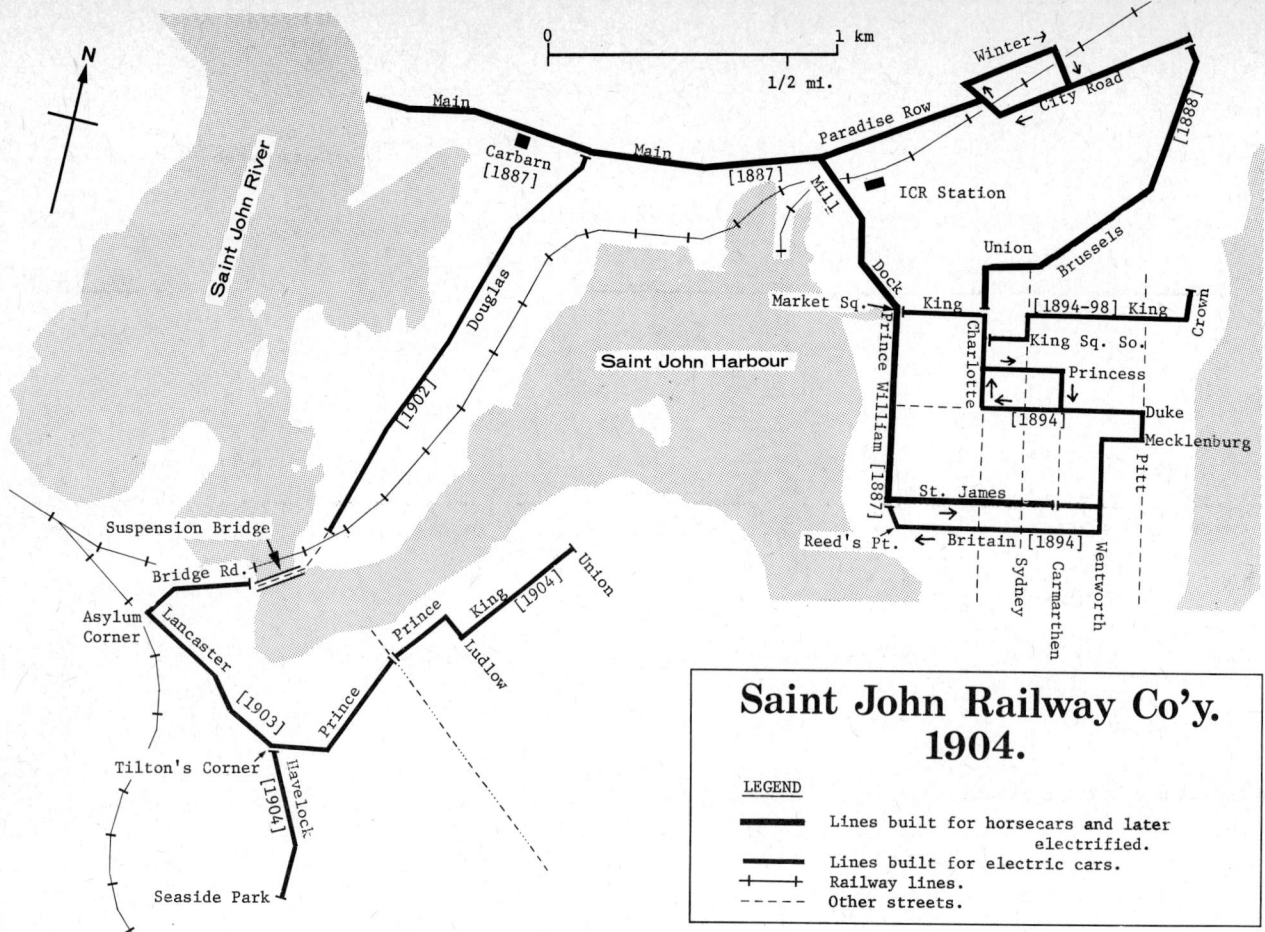

Saint John Railway Co'y. 1904.

LEGEND

━━━━━ Lines built for horsecars and later electrified.
───── Lines built for electric cars.
─┼─┼─ Railway lines.
- - - - Other streets.

Photo below:

Open car No. 49, southbound on Charlotte Street, passing King Square about 1906.

—Wilson Studio.

Photo above:

A view looking up King Street in May, 1899, as car 34 halts on Charlotte Street a block away. The two dogs seem unconcerned about the presence of the cameraman. Note the great height of the telegraph poles—about five storeys.

Photo below:

A view looking down King Street in May, 1899. A Saint John Railway Company closed car is about to climb the steep hill. The street is still unpaved, and the car tracks project above the street level to the chagrin, no doubt, of the carriage drivers.

27

—Collection of the author.

thence via Charlotte, Princess, Carmarthen, Duke, Pitt, Mecklenburg, Wentworth, and Britain streets to Reed's Point, then via Prince William Street to Market Square and so back to Indiantown. The alternate car, on arriving at Market Square would continue along Prince William Street to Reed's Point, then follow St. James, Wentworth, Mecklenburg, Pitt, Duke, and Charlotte streets to the head of King Street, then down the hill to Market Square and back to Indiantown.

The second route was to be a loop line employing four cars, two in either direction. This loop would start at the corner of Paradise Row and Main Street, follow Paradise Row and City Road to Haymarket Square, then via Brussels, Union, Charlotte, King, Dock, and Mill streets to the starting point. The third route was to have used three cars, starting from Paradise Row and Main Street, going via Mill, Dock, King, Charlotte, Union, and Crown streets, returning via King Street East, King, Dock, and Mill streets. This third route, however, was operated in a different form than had been planned, and lasted only a few years. If the reader finds this complicated, a brief study of the map will clarify the picture, and show that the new system would include all the lines of the old

—Canadian Railway Museum.

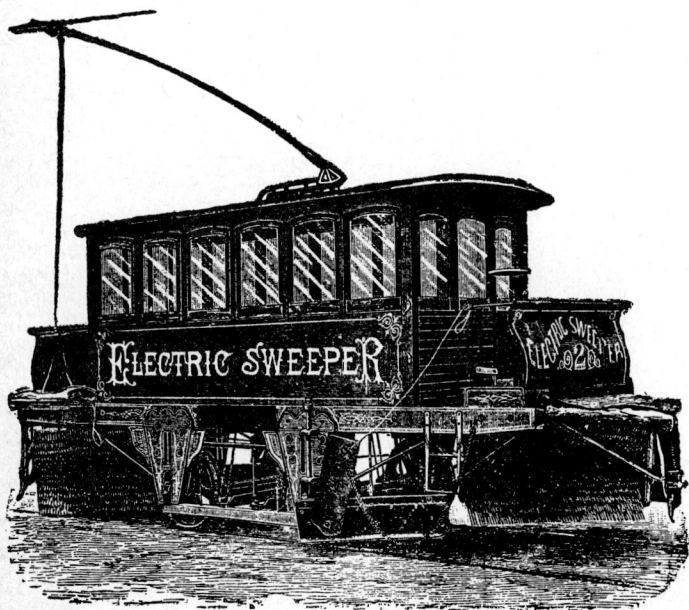

system, as well as cover the city so thoroughly that scarcely any point in central Saint John would be more than two blocks from a car line. The section from Indiantown to Reed's Point would be double track, as would Brussels Street and King Street. At the same time, plans were made for future expansion to the West side and to the beaches, as well as to the rural cemeteries.

Before the end of April, the plans had been approved by the city council despite some argument that certain streets were too narrow for double track. An order was placed in England for 74 lb. "T" rails "capable of carrying the largest CPR or ICR train", and new double-ended cars were ordered from Ahearn & Soper of Ottawa. The Saint John Railway Company promised that it would build a first-class street railway and provide as efficient a service as any system in Canada.

About the middle of July the rails arrived from England and work began almost at once. Construction was carried out under the direction of F.P. Brothers, a former CPR roadmaster who had been present at the driving of the CPR's last spike at Craigellachie, BC in 1885. Ground was broken at the corner of Crown Street and King Street East, and very soon between 350 and 500 men were at work. At first, track was laid on the new lines, leaving the existing routes in operation, still with the old equipment; but, at the rate of 350 to 400 feet per day, it was not long until the old lines were reached too, and, following the completion of the King Street track work, all service was discontinued in August

Above, left:
The only known photograph of a street car on the original King Street East line. The car, one of the ex-Consolidated Electric Company cars, is depicted on King Square South at Charlotte Street, between 1894 and 1899, when this line was abandoned. This photograph establishes that Consolidated Electric cars were operated by the Saint John Railway for a few years after 1894.

Above, centre:
Model of one of the first Saint John Railway electric cars. This model, made in 1896, is actually an inkwell and stood on the desk of General Manager Matthew Neilson. The wheels are Canadian large cents.

Left:
Drawing of the electric sweeper purchased in 1894.
—*Daily Telegraph* December 28th 1894;
Public Archives of Canada, L5836.

28

Drawing of one of the new cars of the Saint John Railway Company as delivered in 1894.
—*Daily Telegraph* September 26th 1894;
Public Archives of Canada, L3271.

while the reconstruction proceeded. Even the overhead wire was replaced, and at the same time, $10,000 was spent to strengthen the car barn to take the weight of the heavier cars, and two new 250 horsepower generators were installed in the enlarged power house. On September 25th, the first seven of eleven new trams arrived on flatcars, and hundreds of people went to see them: The "Daily Telegraph" reported:

"These cars have excited the admiration of all who have seen them. They are about 24 feet in length and are provided with a vestibule at each end so that the driver and conductor will be completely protected from the weather. The interior finish of the car is of mahogany upholstered in English Wilton, with beveled plate glass windows, birds eye veneered ceiling, polished brass trimmings and automatic Pullman car curtains. Each car has a coal stove of the new Gurney style which rests upon the seat in the centre of one side of the cars. The register of fares is operated not by means of a cord as in the old cars but by means of an iron rod to which short levers are attached. Each car is provided with a clock, and the whole aspect of them is most cheerful and comfortable. The new cars will not require to be turned so that neither Y's nor turntables will be necessary, for the motorman can operate them from either end, both ends being alike. This arrangement will save much time and be a great convenience in every way. The new cars will be provided with lifesaving fenders. They rest upon solid iron trucks and have powerful springs, and running on a perfect roadbed they will be entirely free from the jolting and jarring which have made the other cars so uncomfortable. It may be said of these cars that they are equal in appearance and equipment to any cars on any street railway in the United States or Canada. They are handsomely lettered, and the circuit to which they belong is shown by lettered boards on the sides and in front."

These cars were numbered 30 to 40, and served for many years, some lasting until the change to right hand operation in 1922. Until well after 1900 they were the mainstay of the system, and future car orders, also from Ottawa, retained the basic design, with slight modifications, until 1906. The company was so proud of the richly finished interiors, so different from the earlier cars, that they soon installed signs reading: "Please remove your raincoat and leave the seat dry for the next passenger". A new paint scheme of maroon and cream with yellow trim became standard, and was continued until the New Brunswick Power Company introduced an all-red livery in 1917.

By October 18th, work was complete, and Van Horne and Ross announced that no more work would be done that year. The routes were operated as previously outlined except that the third line ran only from Market Square via King Street, and the South side of King Square, then via King Street East, and Crown to Union streets, returning the same way. Only one car was used on this route, usually one of the old Consolidated Electric Company's converted horse cars, and service was very infrequent. On all lines the practice was continued of stopping wherever a passenger hailed a car except that no stops were made while ascending long hills in order to avoid the difficulty of starting on a grade. To supplement route name boards, the cars bore identification signs as follows: Main line cars which turned up King Street carried a green square, while the alternate cars which continued along Prince William Street displayed a red circle. The Paradise Row and Haymarket Square loop line was identified by a white diamond, while the King Street East car carried an orange triangle. Within a few months the Haymarket Square loop line was cut to three cars, operating only from Mill Street via Paradise Row, Haymarket Square, Brussels and Union streets, to the corner of Charlotte and King streets, much as the old cars had done, since it was found that the main line provided adequate service on King, Dock, and Mill streets. The section on Union Street between Brussels and Crown streets was never built, and the King Street East line carried so few passengers that it had been abandoned by 1899.

Open cars Nos. 29 and 41 in Market Square. Car No. 29 was one of the original Ottawa-built cars of 1894, while No. 41 was acquired from Montreal in 1898.
—*Collection of Roy Melvin.*

Car No. 33, one of the Ottawa-built cars of 1894, descends King Street hill in 1906. The building behind the car is the Court House, built in 1827, and now one of the oldest buildings in Saint John.

—Wilson Studio.

By the end of 1894, the Saint John Railway Company was operating an 11½-mile, excellently-built street railway, serving the most populous areas with cars of the most recent construction, supplemented in rush hours by some of the old cars which were retained until about 1900. A fare of 5¢ was charged, and transfers were used for the first time. In November 1894, a new, powerful sweeper arrived from Ahearn & Soper, and was soon busily at work. With the arrival of the sweeper the practice of salting the streets to keep the tracks open was discontinued, not to be resumed until more than half a century later when the great increase of automobile traffic brought about a return to this practice. The first big test of the sweeper came on the night of December 27th, 1894, when a storm, almost as big as that of the preceding January, struck without warning. This time the lines, although more than double their former length, were cleared in a few hours instead of

nearly a week. But in the great storm of March 1895, even the sweeper had little effect on the wet snow, and the line was practically shut for several days. Yet such events were rare, and in the next 54 years there were only about a dozen cases of really serious snow blockage, the worst of all occurring in 1920. The early cars did not have automatic sanders, so on snowy days when the rails were slippery, the company would hire neighbourhood youngsters to ride on the front steps and sprinkle sand on the rails while climbing the hills.

In March 1895, the promise was made that work would begin that spring on the line to the west side, as well as that to the cemetery. Despite these promises and hopes, no further extension was carried out in the Nineteenth Century, and it was not until 1902 that the sound of new street railway construction was heard again in the streets of Saint John.

6

Turn of the Century

*A*FTER THE GREAT changes of 1894, the next few years were relatively quiet with few modifications to the street railway. Gradually the trolleys became part of the way of life of the city, and it was hard to imagine what it would be like without them. To the children, in those days before the automobile, the electric cars were a source of wonder, and the game "Ding! ding!—this car goes up King" was a favourite of youngsters of that generation. The most noteworthy event of 1895 was the Saint John Railway Company's takeover of the gas light company which had been established as far back as 1845. Thus the street railway now controlled both the electric and gas lighting, as well as public transportation in Saint John. Outside the area served by street cars, private omnibuses continued to operate, especially along Douglas Avenue, and across the suspension bridge to the west side. These omnibuses, nicknamed "army worms", were decidedly uncomfortable, so there was some agitation for extension of the electric lines. But the company bided its time and found plausible-sounding excuses for rejecting these pleas.

During this period, several open cars were bought, the first in Saint John, and these soon proved very popular. One of these cars was elaborately decorated with coloured lights and fancy displays to commemorate the Diamond Jubilee (60th anniversary) of Queen Victoria's reign in June 1897, and it toured all of the lines for several evenings during the festivities. The open cars were very well received, and five more were acquired in 1898, along with two closed cars. The new open cars were built by the Montreal Street Railway and were exactly like those built for Montreal in the same year. They had flat canopy roofs and were single-ended, the last "single-enders" to come to Saint John. The arrival of these new cars resulted in the retirement of the last of the old Consolidated Electric Company's equipment, so that as the new century began, no car on the system was more than seven years old.

Up to this time, apart from minor accidents, the company's reputation for safety was excellent, but in 1897 and 1898, two serious runaways occurred on hills and spoiled this record. Car No. 40 was descending Indiantown hill on January 15th 1897, when its brake chain jammed and the car ran out of control off the end of the rails and out onto the wharf. Fortunately, No. 40 was stopped just short of the end of the wharf and was pulled back, without damage, by a chain attached to another car. However, a few more feet and it would have been a different story.

The other runaway, on July 17th 1898, had more serious consequences. Open car No. 41, descending Mill Street, lost control just after crossing Union Street, ran across the CPR tracks at 30 miles an hour, and buried itself ten feet inside a saloon, scattering the saloon keeper's cash receipts far and wide. In this case, it was proved that the car had been knowingly operated with defective brakes, and damages of $25,000 were awarded to the injured persons. After these accidents, a few cars were fitted with emergency brakes with a double ratchet, working equally well in either direction. These eventually became standard, but not until the coming of one-man cars after 1920. About the same time, numerous encounters with pedestrians—none fatal, fortunately—prompted the design of a new type of fender. This consisted of a "platform" of bed spring construction, projecting four feet in front of the car at a height of three inches above the rails. This, although better, was not entirely satisfactory. It was replaced, eventually about 1906, with a more elaborate folding design which became the standard type used until 1948.

By the turn of the century the agitation for a line to the west side was becoming too great to be ignored. The first proposal was for a single track line along Douglas Avenue, branching off the main line and extending to the suspension bridge; in 1899, the city council approved the

building of this line. By that year, the rails had been taken up from the King Street East line and speculation was that they would be re-laid on Douglas Avenue. However, winter came and nothing was done, largely because the city insisted that the company pay $10,000 of the expenses of re-grading the street. At length, a compromise was reached in the spring of 1902, and after considerable debate, the use of 74 lb. "T" rail was approved, meaning that work could start immediately using the existing stock of rail. Actual construction began on May 14th 1902, with completion scheduled for July 1st. But difficulty was experienced with the curved sections and special work, and night shifts were put on to speed up the job. Although the track construction was adequate, the condition of the recently filled-in roadbed soon caused the rails to sink in spots, giving a rougher ride than on other parts of the system; this was still notice-able forty years later. The line was finally opened on July 21st, when two closed cars

began to shuttle between Main Street and the bridge, at ten-minute intervals. Although the cars were often crowded, the old omnibuses still continued, since their passengers were usually bound for the west side where the street cars still did not run.

The very fact of the opening of the new line quickly awakened memories of the still-unfull-filled promises made in 1894. In July 1902, editorials appeared in several newspapers highly critical of the street railway and its monopoly, describing all the extensions and improvements that had been promised but were still not built. It was pointed out that the company had pro-mised to give Saint John a street car service second to none; now, eight years later, it was far from this goal, since the cars were too few and the lines too short. The charge was made that "The railway clings to the streets where the nickels are the thickest and goes in for easy dividends". Great criticism was levelled at the

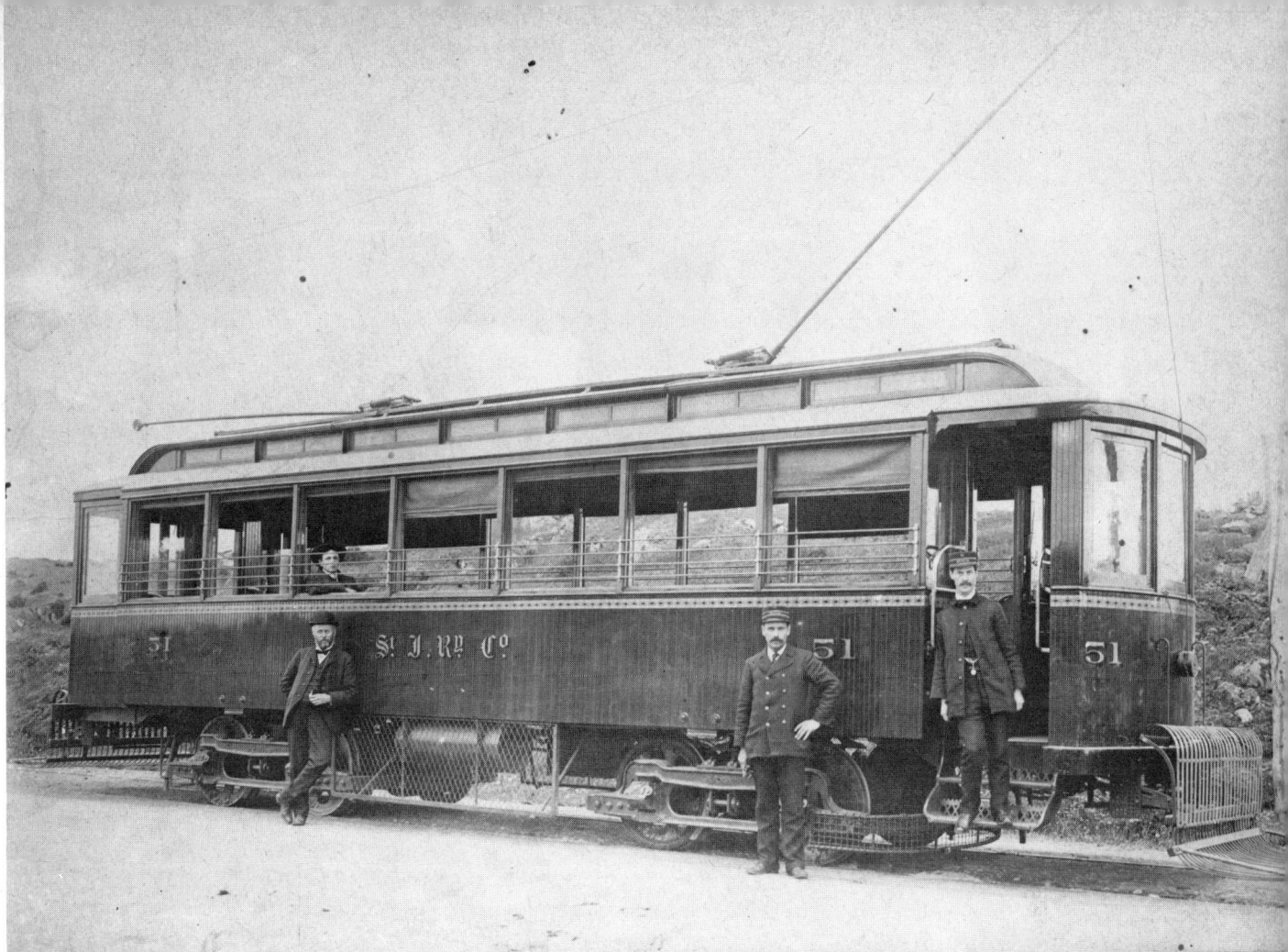

city council of 1894 for giving away valuable concessions so easily, and demands were made that the company either build its extensions or the city should expropriate the street railway and run it as a municipal department. No doubt much of this criticism was unfounded, but some was undoubtedly true, especially the reference to too few cars at peak travel times. It was often charged that Saint John with 12 miles of track and 22 cars had operated only 445,667 car miles in 1901, compared with Halifax which operated 612,149 car miles with eight miles of track. This ill will towards the street railway was heightened two years later when the company "arrogantly" refused to introduce special workman's fares, or put on extra cars at the time of the Champlain Tercentenary celebrations of 1904. For some years threats were made to petition the Legislature to cancel the rights granted in 1894, but this agitation gradually subsided, and the 1894 agreement continued as the basis for operation until 1948.

Above, this page:

Double truck car No. 51, just delivered from Montreal, is depicted showing the crew and company officers standing alongside. The year was 1903.

Photo opposite:

Sister cars, Nos. 32 and 33, side by side at Indiantown. No. 33 has just arrived from downtown Saint John, while No. 32 is about to start the return trip. Note the route indicators above the signs. This photograph was taken in 1906, when Indiantown was still the terminus of the main line. The steamer wharf and Saint John River are in the background.

How much of an effect this dissatisfaction had is difficult to determine, but the fact is that— starting with the summer of 1902, possibly under threat of civic expropriation or competition—the company began to adopt a much more progressive policy towards the building of new lines. Under the able guidance of General Manager Neilson, plans were made for the long-awaited extensions to Carleton on the west side of the harbour. Schedules were speeded up, and fixed car stops were arranged, abolishing the old practice of stopping wherever a passenger hailed a car. New blue-and-white enamelled route signs replaced the old boards, and the cars were repainted and generally made more attractive. Early in 1903, new cars were delivered, the first since 1898. These comprised six double-truck cars obtained second-hand from the Montreal Park and Island Railway in Montreal. They had been built in 1900, and were of the semi-convertible design with cross seats, were double-ended, and were equipped with air brakes. Numbered 50 to 55, they were placed in service on the Douglas Avenue line, as they were too large to clear on all curves on the other lines. They were the only double-truck cars, or cars with air brakes, ever used in Saint John; they lasted barely five years, three being sold in 1908 to Berlin (now Kitchener), Ontario and the other three to Lévis, Quebec. Due to this new progressive policy, 1902 began a period of expansion of the Saint John Railway which was to continue for the next fifteen years, the period of the great days of the trolley in North America.

ST. JOHN TO SEASIDE PARK

TROLLEY TRIPS

7

Years of Expansion

IN THE SPRING of 1903, agreements were made between the Saint John Railway Company and the city and county authorities for the building and operating of street railways on the west side of the harbour. Examination of the ageing suspension bridge quickly disclosed that it would not be feasible to run street cars across it without spending considerable sums in strengthening the structure. Since the bridge was fifty years old and slated for replacement, it was decided not to attempt to connect the west side lines with the east except by a free transfer, passengers walking across the bridge to board the cars on the other side. Arrangements were made with the CPR for the movement of cars over the adjacent railway bridge when it was necessary to transfer the equipment from one side to the other, although this was seldom necessary since maintenance facilities were provided on the west side as well. This arrangement continued until the present highway bridge went into service in 1916.

During 1903 a line was built from the west side of the bridge to Lancaster Heights Road, down that road to Tilton's Corner, then down Prince Street to the Saint John city line. At this point a dispute with the city halted work and prevented the proposed extension to the ferry landing at Rodney wharf until the following year. Also in 1903 the Douglas Avenue line was double-tracked to carry the extra traffic, although the somewhat unsatisfactory foundation remained and the condition of the track suffered accordingly. In 1904 the west side line was extended down Prince Street into the Carleton region of Saint John, and terminated at Rodney Street not far from the ferry landing.

That spring the company purchased a thirteen-acre lot on the shore of the bay, built an amusement park known as Seaside Park, and constructed a car line from Tilton's Corner to reach it. The idea of a park run by the street railway had been planned as far back as 1893 in the days of the Consolidated Electric Company,

which had been given expropriation rights for this purpose, but nothing had been done for more than ten years. This park was opened July 1st 1904, and the first few weekends of operation the cars were so crowded that people had long waits just to get aboard, causing the usual complaints of inadequate service. Later, however, sufficient extra cars were put on to handle the crowds. This line is still fondly remembered by older residents who recall the summer rides on the open cars to the amusement park and beach, and the equally enjoyable return journeys at the end of an exciting and happy outing. A large pavilion was erected at Seaside Park, and four street cars could run right inside for the convenience of the thousands of persons who flocked there on fine summer days. The extension of the street cars into the west side finally displaced the old omnibusses which thereafter were confined to Millidgeville and some other areas not served by trolleys.

In 1905 a rearrangement of the track in the central part of Saint John was made when the line up Princess Street was extended, with 90 lb. rail, to Wentworth Street, then north to King Street East, east to Pitt Street, and along Pitt and Britain streets to Wentworth. The two-block section on Carmarthen street between Princess and Duke streets was abandoned, and the south end loop operated over this extended route. No further changes were made to the basic track layout in the centre of the city during the days of the electric cars.

Opposite page, upper:

The men who operated the cars. A group of photographs of all of the motormen and conductors on the Saint John Railway in 1903. The gentleman depicted just below car No. 51 is Matthew Neilson, the general manager from 1896 to 1903.

—R.D. Thomas Collection.

Opposite page, lower:

A 1904 post card with views of Saint John superimposed on a stylized street car advertising rides to Seaside Park. No car like this ever ran in Saint John!

—New Brunswick Museum.

—Wilson Studio (above, and bottom photo).

—Roy Melvin Collection.

Later in 1905 an issue arose which threatened to have serious consequences affecting all privately-owned street railways in Canada. The act of 1894 had included certain agreements between the company and the city regarding the maintenance of streets occupied by street car tracks. One of the major clauses required the company to maintain the street between the rails and eighteen inches either side of them; but by a subsequent deal, made in 1897, the city had agreed to accept $7,000 per year in lieu of this maintenance. The city council of 1905, however, felt much less kindly to the street railway than the council in 1894, and as a result of their efforts, the Provincial Legislature passed an act requiring, among other things, the company to maintain the entire street from curb to curb. This act was hailed as a very dangerous piece of legislation which in effect sanctioned a unilateral breaking of a contract by one of the parties thereto, and constituted a serious threat to the street railway industry in general. After further consideration, the Legislature realized the consequences and repealed the offending act, but controversy between the city and the company continued as long as the street cars ran.

Work on the West Saint John lines started on April 18th 1906 and continued during that year and 1907, as a new track was laid from the bridge road to Barnhill's corner at Clark Street in Fairville. In Carleton, the original line was double-tracked and a loop line created by the construction of track on Winslow, Tower, Queen, and Union streets (West) to the ferry wharf, with a spur extending along the wharf affording connection to the ferry, and a transfer to the Prince William Street line on the other side of the harbour. This loop remained intact only until the outbreak of World War I, when military security compelled the abandonment of the section on Queen Street and along the docks. Improvements were also carried out in the centre of the city by the opening of a track from Union Street to Charlotte via Sydney Street and King Square, and at this time also, Paradise Row and City Road were double-tracked.

This page, upper:

King Street East, looking eastward from Wentworth in 1906. The countryside on the other side of Courtenay Bay was still rural, in strong contrast to today!

This page, centre:

Boston Elevated Railway car No. 551 as pictured in Boston about 1906. Four identical cars were sold to Saint John in 1908.

This page, left:

Open car No. 83 heading towards downtown Saint John about 1912. Note the crossover in the background. This car was rebuilt as a closed car in 1927 and it survived until 1948.

Opposite page, upper:

On a crisp, bright winter day in 1914, car No. 44 crosses Market Square. Winter road travel was still by sleigh, with automobiles only in evidence during summer when roads were best.

Opposite page, right:

Open car No. 41 going up King Street about 1906. The buildings on the left were demolished in 1974 to make way for a new development.

—Wilson Studio (both photos).

To keep pace with this extension and improvement of service, new equipment was required, and several purchases of cars, both open and closed, were made between 1903 and 1907, so by that year there were 21 closed and 20 open cars running in Saint John.

During the period of almost six years, from 1906 through 1911, there is no record that the company bought any cars new. However, possibly for reasons of economy, a variety of second-hand cars were purchased from Boston, Buffalo and other US cities. Most of these cars, some dating back as far as 1892, did not last long in Saint John, and were confined largely to rush hour service. For the next few years, no new lines were built, but two private organisations sought to build car lines in the Saint John area. One plan, launched in 1906, called for a line on Adelaide Avenue from Main Street to Millidgeville on the Kennebecasis river, a distance of 3½ miles. The group sought running rights over the Saint John Railway to King Street, but was unable to obtain financial support and the plan died after a few months. The idea of a Millidgeville line was several times considered by the street railway, but it was never built. Even more ephemeral was the plan to build a suburban road twelve miles to Westfield, — obviously merely a hoax to inflate land values in the area. The truth of the matter was that the state of the money market following the financial panic of 1907 was not conducive to street railway construction either by the existing company or by newcomers to the business, and several years had to pass until the next stage of expansion came about.

Car No. 106, the first of a group of twelve cars, loaded on a Canadian Pacific flatcar at Tillsonburg, Ontario, for the 1000-mile trip to Saint John.

By 1911 the general financial situation had improved, and street car lines in North America were growing rapidly again; their last period of great expansion. Since the last track construction, in 1907, the Saint John Railway had experimented with "Pay-as-you-enter" cars, and this method of fare collection was shortly to be employed on most of the closed cars. There was even talk of one-man cars, but this scheme was not to come about for another ten years since wages had not yet risen to a point where one-man operation was necessary. In October 1911, the company increased the wages of its motormen and conductors by 1¢ per hour, the new rates being 18½¢ per hour for new employees, ranging up to 21¢ for five-year veterans, with 3¢ extra on Sundays. In 1911 also, plans were drawn up for new car lines branching off at Haymarket Square, and extending to the north and east. One line was to extend to Fernhill cemetery, and another was to go to the east side of Courtenay Bay where a new residential area was springing up. There was even talk of a line parallel to the Intercolonial Ry. (now CNR) tracks to Rothesay in King's County, a residential village about eight miles from Saint John. Final agreements were made during 1912, but little actual construction was done.

At this time, the "Main line" cars began to be routed along Douglas Avenue to the bridge, with alternate cars going to the Indiantown loop. Work began on a new carbarn, of modern construction, on Wentworth Street, a much more central location. Adjacent to the new barn, repair shops were erected; in these shops, in later days, cars were not only completely rebuilt, but ten cars were built new in Wentworth shops in the 1920s. When the new car barn and shops were completed, in 1913, the old structure on Main Street was relegated to the storage of old

The crew poses proudly beside car No. 84, resplendent in fresh paint, newly delivered from the Ottawa Car company in December 1912. This was one of six cars which were the first in Saint John to be newly-built as pay-as-you-enter cars. Later rebuilt, all survived until the end of service in 1948.

—Wilson Studio.

and little-used cars. In 1912, definite plans were made for a new 730-foot bridge across the Reversing Falls, which would allow the two sections of the street railway to be connected, so eliminating a major bottleneck.

In February 1912, the company ordered, from the Ottawa Car Company, the first Saint John cars especially designed for "Pay-as-you-enter" operation. These six cars, the 80 series of even numbers, were 32 feet long, having 21-foot bodies and wide entrance doors. These trams, the largest single-truck cars yet run in Saint John, were the last from the Ottawa Car Company and the last with clerestory roofs. The first three, probably 80, 82 and 84, were delivered late in November 1912 and the other three followed by the beginning of 1913. With subsequent rebuilding, these cars lasted until the end of street car service.

Tracklaying began from Haymarket Square, across the Marsh bridge along what is now Thorne Avenue to Kane's Corner in the spring of 1913. At the same time, a branch was built on Rothesay Avenue to the "One Mile House", as well as a connecting line along Russell Street from Kane's corner to One Mile House. The first car reached Kane's corner on November 11th, 1913, and the loop via Russell Street was first used on December 12th, 1913. Operation on the Russell Street track lasted only two years, until the Rothesay Avenue line was extended to Glen Falls. In March 1913, the company received permission from the Provincial Legislature to extend its lines into King's County, so paving the way for the proposed extension to Rothesay.

To serve the new lines, both built and proposed, new cars were needed; early in 1914 an order was placed with the Tillsonburg Electric Car Company of Tillsonburg, Ontario for twelve cars. These, the first arch roofed closed cars in Saint John, were delivered that spring, and presented a singularly different appearance with their arch windows and vertical tongue-and-groove sheathing. This order was one of only three the Tillsonburg company ever received, as it went out of business the same year. Even-numbered 106-128, the "Tillsonburg cars" were later steel-sheathed and fitted with more conventional windows, but they lasted 34 years, until the end of street cars in Saint John.

In the meantime, another corporation had entered the field. On April 20th, 1912, the New Brunswick Hydro-Electric Company had been incorporated with the object of building power dams and facilities to supply electric power to parts of New Brunswick including Saint John. While no mention was made of electric railways, the promoters evidently had them in mind, for the next year the same promoters started the Saint John Suburban Railway Company, which was duly organized and incorporated in April 1913. This new company was empowered to build suburban railways in the Saint John area, operated by electricity, steam, gasoline, or other power, provided it did not infringe the rights of the Saint John Railway Company, and did not collect fares in areas served by the older company. These were the days of rosy visions by electric railway promoters, and the plans for the

suburban railway fully exemplified these visions. It was proposed to build lines to: Loch Lomond (10 miles), Rothesay (8 miles), Millidgeville (3 miles), and Westfield (14 miles). Surveys were begun, but no construction took place, and the outbreak of war the following year brought an end to both the plans of the suburban railway, and the era of major electric railway expansion. However, the New Brunswick Hydro-Electric Company remained in existence and was very soon renamed the New Brunswick Power Company eventually buying the street railway in Saint John.

Early in the summer of 1914 the Saint John Railway Company suffered its first serious labour dispute, and the events of that July were among the most violent incidents ever to occur in Saint John. In mid-July, a conductor named Ramsey was discharged for leaving a car while on duty and allowing the motorman to proceed without him. This created ill-will among the employees which reached a high pitch on July 17th, when four motormen and four conductors were discharged for not stopping at the steam railway crossings. After much angry but futile talk, the men voted in favour of a strike, and about 100 employees accordingly walked out on July 22nd. The company continued to operate some cars using employees who refused to strike, and by temporary employees hired for the occasion. Meanwhile, the strikers organized an impromptu jitney bus service, one of the first in Canada. Tempers flared high. The climax came on July 24th at Market Square. An angry crowd had collected, and as car No. 84 began to cross the square it was surrounded by the mob, most of which had little direct interest in the strike, but were out for some excitement. The passengers hastily disembarked, and a shower of bricks and paving stones soon smashed all

the car windows. Car 71, close behind, met a similar fate, but the mob was not yet satisfied. Strong ropes were soon produced and attached to the cars, and, to the accompaniment of shouts of encouragement, both 84 and 71 were toppled over on their sides. The whole situation was now out of control, and when the mob attacked the powerhouse and sabotaged the generators the city was plunged into darkness. An attack on the new Wentworth Street car barn was repulsed as the barn was nearly a mile from the centre of the action, and the mob's strength was diminished by the time it reached there. At any rate, most of the rioters stayed in the Market Square area. The mayor read the Riot Act, and the army was called in to restore order after two policemen had been thrown through a plate glass window. The outcome was a full fledged cavalry charge, complete with swords (ceremonial, and thus, fortunately flat-edged) down King Street and into the mob. The "battle" which followed was more or less of a draw, but the soldiers retired with several casualties.

This page, above:

Cars Nos. 71 and 84, stoned and overturned by rioters in Market Square in July 1914. Both cars were subsequently repaired, and No. 84 lasted until 1948.
—New Brunswick Museum.

Opposite page, upper:

A closeup of car No. 71 showing the damaged fender, and onlookers peering through the glassless windows.
—Gorham Photo Services.

Opposite page, right:

A sweeper clears the track on Prince William Street during a blizzard about 1910, while shovel-bearing workers stand aside to let it pass. The vacant lot behind the sleigh in the background became the site of the post office.
—New Brunswick Museum.

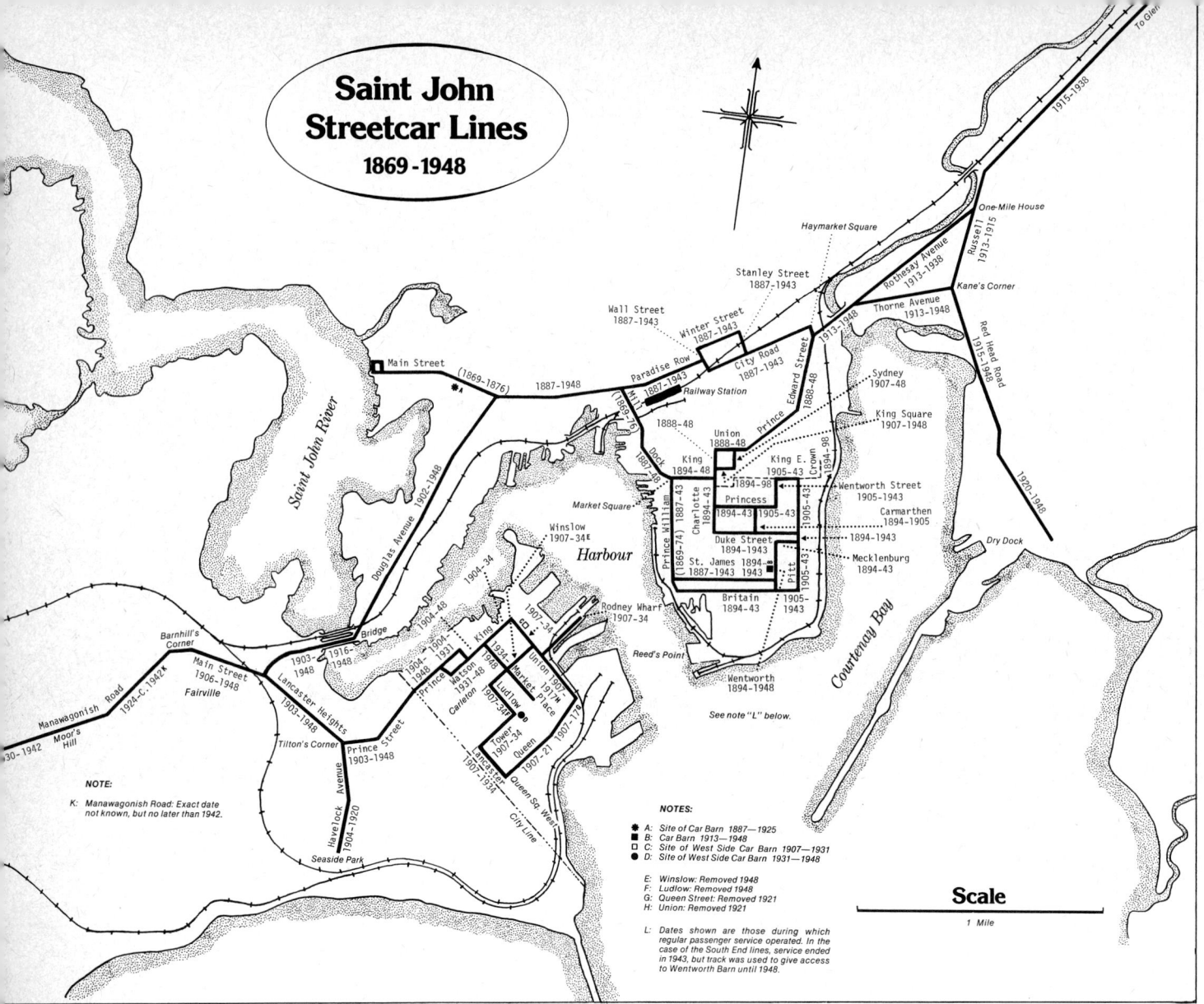

Saint John Streetcar Lines
1869-1948

To Glen

1915-1938

One-Mile House

Russell 1913-1915

Rothesay Avenue 1913-1938

Kane's Corner

Haymarket Square

Stanley Street 1887-1943

Thorne Avenue 1913-1948

Red Head Road 1915-1948

Wall Street 1887-1943

Winter Street 1887-1943

Paradise Row

City Road 1887-1943

1913-1948

Main Street (1869-1876)

1887-1948

1887-1943

Railway Station

Saint John River

Douglas Avenue 1902-1948

1888-48

Sydney 1907-48

King Square 1907-1948

Prince Edward Street

1888-48

Union 1888-48

King 1894-48

King E. 1905-43

Crown 1894-98

Wentworth Street 1905-1943

1920-1948

Market Square

Dock

1894-98

Charlotte 1894-43

Carmarthen 1894-1905

Prince William (1869-74) 1887-1943

Princess 1894-43

1905-43

1894-1903

Mecklenburg 1894-43

Dry Dock

Winslow 1907-34 E

Harbour

Duke Street 1894-1943

1905-43

1894-1943

St. James 1894- 1887-1943 1943

Britain 1894-43

Pitt

1905-1943

Courtenay Bay

Barnhill's Corner

1904-34

Rodney Wharf 1907-34

Reed's Point

Bridge

1903- 1916- 1948 1948

1904-48

Main Street 1906-1948

Fairville

Lancaster Heights 1903-1948

1904- 1931

Prince

Watson 1931-48

King

1924- 1948

Union 1907-1917

1907-34

See note "L" below.

Wentworth 1894-1948

Manawagonish Road 1924-C.1942 K

Moor's Hill

Tilton's Corner 1903-1948

Prince Street 1903-1948

Carleton 1907-34

Market Place

Ludlow 1907-34 F D

Tower 1907-54

Queen 1907-21 1907-34

1830- 1942

Havelock Avenue 1904-1920

Lancaster 1907-1934

Queen Sq. West

City Line

Seaside Park

NOTE:

K: Manawagonish Road: Exact date not known, but no later than 1942.

NOTES:

* A: Site of Car Barn 1887—1925
■ B: Car Barn 1913—1948
□ C: Site of West Side Car Barn 1907—1931
● D: Site of West Side Car Barn 1931—1948

E: Winslow: Removed 1948
F: Ludlow: Removed 1948
G: Queen Street: Removed 1921
H: Union: Removed 1921

L: Dates shown are those during which regular passenger service operated. In the case of the South End lines, service ended in 1943, but track was used to give access to Wentworth Barn until 1948.

Scale
1 Mile

The next day the army's strength had risen to 500, and after waiting most of the day, in the evening the order was given to clear the streets. By now, common sense was returning, the order was carried out with little difficulty, and the next day the strike was over. The discharged employees were not re-hired, but the company granted recognition to the employees' union. In the next few days, operation of the street railway returned to normal, and scarcely a week later the street car strike was largely forgotten as ominous news bulletins told of the rapid deterioration of the troubled political situation in Europe. Events there quickly went from bad to worse, and within a few days most of Europe and the British Empire, including Canada, were active belligerents in the first World War.

Saint John, an important seaport, was soon actively involved in the war, as countless ships sailed during the next four years, carrying men and supplies to unknown destinations "somewhere overseas". Nevertheless, despite the war, work did continue, albeit somewhat slowly, on the proposed extensions of the street railway. In October 1914, tracklaying began on the continuation of the line from One Mile House, out along the side of the highway towards suburban Glen Falls, and to the Maynor House, a large dance pavilion. Sixty-two-foot-long 80 lb. rails were used on this section, and the "Three Mile House" near Coldbrook station was reached on

May 24th 1915. By July 1st, track had reached Glen Falls, and complete service began that day. This line was very popular for outings, and on occasion eight cars were run from King Street to carry the crowds. Operation was discontinued on the cutoff along Russell Street, and a few years later the tracks were taken up. The line from Kane's Corner was extended along the Red Head road in East Saint John, then still quite rural, and on August 19th 1915, it reached its terminus, about half a mile from where the drydock is today.

At this time there was a dispute with the city concerning the old problem of girder rail versus "T" rail. Certain sections of track had been removed for maintenance, and the city refused to allow them to be replaced unless with girder rail and concrete foundations. Various interpretations were made of the provisions of the act of 1887, and the matter was taken to the New Brunswick Supreme Court. Meanwhile, in two places where the company was re-laying the older type rails, city crews physically tore up the rails and paved the street. A temporary injunction soon permitted the company to continue operation, and early in 1916 the matter was settled by the agreement that the company would pay $5,000 per mile for the city to build new foundations where necessary, and the use of "T" rail was allowed to continue.

In 1915, the new arch bridge over the Reversing Falls was completed, carrying street car track and overhead wire. It is shown at centre, between the 1853 suspension bridge, on the right, which it superseded, and the 1885 railway bridge on the left, which was itself replaced in 1921.
—New Brunswick Museum.

During 1915, work had been proceeding on the new bridge across the Reversing Falls, built by the Dominion Bridge Company, under contract with the Provincial Government, and by the end of the year it was ready for use. The bridge was opened on January 1st 1916, and the first street car crossed on that day. At first there was still a gap between the rail ends at the East end of the bridge, but within a few days a crossing had been installed over the CPR tracks, the gap had been closed, and, for the first time, trolleys could run through to West Saint John direct. The transfer privilege across the ferry was discontinued, and during 1916 the 63-year-old suspension bridge was torn down.

Photo above:

Looking eastward on Main Street from Douglas Avenue in 1918. Car 90 is the last of the 80 series, while two Tillsonburg cars also appear. Note the poster advertising Theda Bara in "The Forbidden Path". This film was made in 1918, the year of the photograph.

—Wilson Studio.

Photo left:

The new arch bridge was opened on January 1st 1916, and street cars crossed for the first time. In the foreground is a former Boston car (probably No. 560), acquired in 1908. The car farthest away is No. 102, bought from Buffalo in 1913, while the one in the middle is an Ottawa Car product of about 1904. The track at the near end is not yet connected, as the level crossing of the CPR track was not installed for several days.

—Wilson Studio.

By 1916 the company had eighteen miles of street railway in operation, but it was feeling the effects of increased prices due to the war, which was now in its third year. The extensions of 1914 and 1915 had been carried out at a considerable financial loss, and, as 1917 came, the future did not look good. There was no longer any talk of new lines, and the ever-increasing numbers of private automobiles promised more and more to threaten existing routes. Since the street railway was no longer a well-paying proposition, the directors began seriously to consider selling the enterprise, and the New Brunswick Power Company (formerly the New Brunswick Hydro-Electric Co.) appeared to be the most logical buyer. On February 3rd, the New Brunswick Investments Company, which had been incorporated only the day before, representing the New Brunswick Power Company, made a bid of $1,300,000 for all the assets, property, and franchises of the Saint John Railway Company. This offer was accepted by a majority of the shareholders, and, by the end of February 1917, the transfer was made, and the New Brunswick Power Company assumed full control of the street railway, power system, and all the street railway franchises in Saint John. The years of expansion were over, apart from a few small extensions in the early twenties, and within little more than a decade the motor bus would begin to displace the electric cars.

8

The Coming
of One-Man Cars

WHEN THE New Brunswick Power Company assumed control of the street railway, the transition to the new management was made smoothly from an operating point of view, since most of the employees retained their old positions and carried on as before. But in corporate circles there were demands for investigation into the details regarding the transfer of the assets of the Saint John Railway Company in an effort to uncover alleged irregularities. Authority for this investigation was granted by the Legislature in 1918, and a commission was set up. The investigation, various charges and counter charges dragged on for more than two years and eventually petered out as it appeared that even if irregularities had been committed they were minor.

By 1918, the old argument about maintenance of streets on which tracks were laid was boiling again. The city contended that rising costs had made the previously-agreed figure of $5,000 per mile inadequate, and felt anyway that the city should take over the street railway, power, and gas system. The whole matter was deferred, late in 1918, and was never really settled, but cropped up from time to time as long as the street cars ran. By 1918, wartime conditions had driven costs, especially wages, up to such a point that the company was finding it hard to make ends meet, even though the cars were carrying 6,000,000 passengers per year. This was double the figure for 1907, and the automobile was not yet a serious competitor. Accordingly, in the spring of 1918, the company put into effect the first fare increase in Saint John's history. Fares went up from six for 25¢ to 6¢ cash, and transfers were sold for 1¢ instead of being free.

Despite this increase, the company tried other measures to economize, including severe curtailment of the number of cars operated. Since 1911, the number of passengers carried per year had increased by 50%, but the car miles were practically the same, about 1,000,000 per year. This was not due to any shortage of equipment, since, in 1919, the New Brunswick Power Company possessed no less than 72 pieces of rolling stock, made up of 46 closed and 26 open cars. This polyglot assortment of equipment included some of the original Saint John Railway cars, dating back to 1894, as well as a variety of ancient second hand cars bought between 1900 and 1911, many of which had not turned a wheel for years. It is evident, therefore, that little scrapping had been done for ten years, the company preferring to keep the old units in storage for parts or possible emergency use. Of these 72 cars, barely 30 were in regular use. Late in 1919, the committee of public safety called attention to the unbelievable overcrowding of the cars in rush hours. It was a normal sight to see passengers hanging from the open doors, and it is said that occasionally some hung from the car sides and even climbed on the roof! The company replied that the only answer to the cost problem was to introduce one-man cars, and, in 1920, the first definite steps in this direction were taken.

Upper photo:
Two Tillsonburg cars appear in this 1916 view taken on Charlotte Street. One car is turning down King, while the other heads south to Princess Street. Automobiles are becoming more and more a part of the urban scene.

Lower photo:
Another scene at the same place, but looking in the opposite direction, and two years later, 1918. The southbound tram is a Tillsonburg, while car No. 71 turns down King.

—Wilson Studio.

Just as all this discussion was coming to a head the system was hit by the worst natural disaster in its history. On February 7th and 8th 1920, a near-record fall of wet snow occurred and soon brought traffic to a standstill. The sweepers and ploughs were powerless against this wet, dense snow. When the snow turned to rain the water and slush flooded the tracks and caused the motors to burn out on all but eight of the cars. Full service was not restored until the end of February, and the loss to the company was more than $40,000 necessitating the omission of the dividend on the preferred stock.

Early in 1920, T.H. McCauley, who had been superintendent of the Calgary Municipal Railway since 1909, became the general manager of the New Brunswick Power Company and soon announced plans for drastic changes in operation. The most important part of the new plan was to introduce single-ended one-man cars of the design which Mr. McCauley had developed for Calgary, and which were extensively used there and in Regina. The Fairville line was to be extended along the Manawagonish Road to Manchester's Corner, and the East Saint John line was to be extended 3,000 feet to the drydock. Also, numerous small changes were to be made to accommodate single-end operation.

The proposal to use one-man cars met with much opposition from the employees' union, on the alleged grounds of safety; when McCauley refused to sign the new wage agreement unless the men agreed to one-man cars, a strike almost took place. After much arguing, an agreement was reached by which the company would fit up two cars for one-man operation, demonstrate them, and ask the city council to approve regular use of one-man cars. Cars 84 and 114 were selected to be the "guinea pigs", and these soon emerged from the shops with two doors on the front left hand side, and the rear door semi-permanently closed up. One of the front doors was of the peculiar "corner" pattern designed by McCauley, so familiar to Calgarians during the later electric era in that city. As a safety precaution, the rear brake, formerly operated by the conductor, was brought forward to the motorman's end as an emergency brake.

The operating platform of car 114 as it appeared when fitted with the McCauley door.
—Wilson Studio.

On July 16th 1920, the first trial trip of a one-man car was made for the city council. This car was driven by the superintendent, Hazen McLean, who had driven the earliest electric car in 1893, and who, incidentally, was on hand for the last run in 1948. After some consideration, the city council ruled that this arrangement of one-man cars was not sufficiently safe, and the result was that two-man cars continued to provide all the service, 84 and 114 being placed in storage.

The extension of the Fairville line was not carried out until 1924, but the East Saint John route was continued out about half a mile to the drydock in 1920, using the rails and wire from the Seaside Park line, abandoned that year. The construction of a loop at Glen Falls completed new trackwork for 1920. Late in 1920, after less than one year, T.H. McCauley resigned as general manager, and with him went the schemes for single-end operation, double-end cars continuing until the end.

By 1921 it was obvious that one-man cars would have to come soon or the system could not continue to operate. Hourly wages now ranged from 49¢ to 55¢ — an increase of 150% in the preceding ten years, while fares had risen only 25%. Early in 1921, the post-World War I boom had begun to fade, and prices were dropping, so the company proposed a 20% wage decrease, later modified to 15%, and finally received city approval to run one-man cars after making some safety modifications.

The first regular one-man cars, Nos. 84 and 114, were demonstrated on June 16th, and went into service before the end of the month. Immediately, most of the men went on strike, and service was much reduced. Remembering the violence of 1914, the city requested protection from the Mounted Police, but some violence still occurred as "goon squads" attacked the street cars. By July 5th, all service was stopped, and a limited jitney operation was being run by the strikers. However the company hired some non-union workers and resumed about one-third of the service on July 10th. Conversion to one-man cars was speeded up, and five were running by July 13th. During the night of July 11th 1921, the most violent episode of the strike took place when a mob tore up about 100 feet of track in Queen Square, West Saint John. This track had been laid in 1907 as a temporary measure on condition that it be removed by 1912, and since then it had been a bone of contention, since it ran right across the centre of the square. After 1921, the track was not replaced, the service being cut short to that extent.

Photos opposite page:

Cars Nos. 84 and 114 fitted up with the McCauley patent corner door, an experiment in one-man operation. These official photographs were taken outside the Wentworth barn. While this door system was not used and both cars were soon altered to more conventional layout, the entire fleet was changed to one-man configuration in 1921.
—Wilson Studio, both photographs.

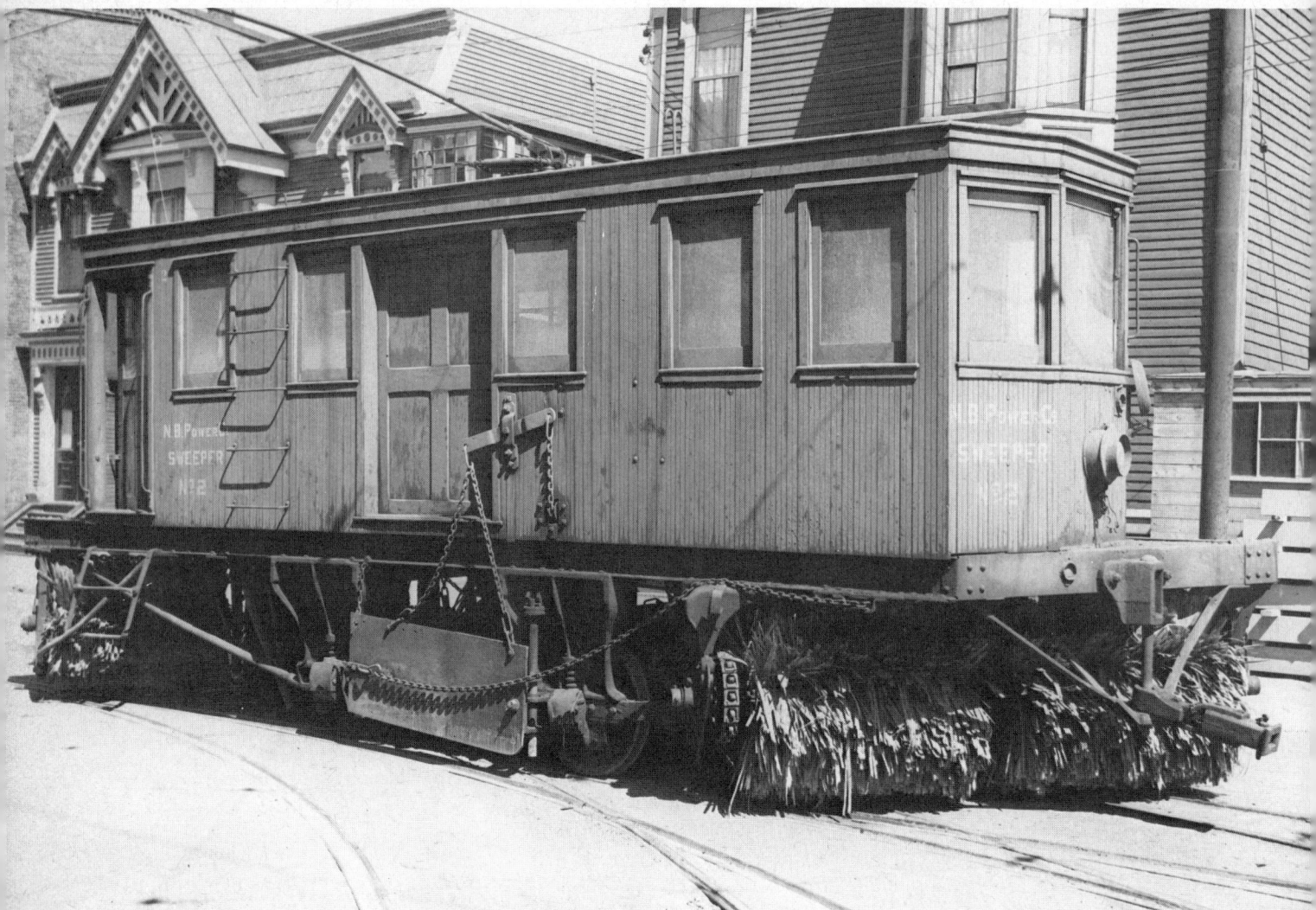

No snow today, as Sweeper No. 2 has its picture taken beside Wentworth barn on May 20th 1946. However, two more winters of service were still ahead.

—M.D. McCarter.

Gradually, order was restored although isolated incidents occurred until the end of the summer. One night someone greased the rails on Indiantown hill, and a car nearly repeated the runaway of 1897, but, as more and more cars returned to service, things got back to normal. The jitney, run by the strikers, became the "Union Bus Company" which carried on for a time but, late in 1921, stopped operation after a court injunction halted this competition. As a result of all these events, about 40 men were dropped from the payroll and 33 of the old cars were scrapped in 1920 and 1921. The total roster at the end of 1921 consisted of 33 closed and 6 open cars, but the open cars were seldom used, and were eventually converted to closed cars. A further fare increase to three tickets for 25¢ or 10¢ cash was made, and a $1.00 unlimited weekly pass came into being. The latter proved very successful, and was an important factor in killing the bus competition. Within a year, 60% of the passengers used the weekly pass, and this continued until the end of tram service, then being adopted by the succeeding bus company. By the start of 1922, the one-man cars had taken over completely, and the whole operation was on a much sounder footing, having passed successfully through one of its worst crises.

A drawing of car No. 88.

—Robert Halfyard.

50

9

Modernization and Rehabilitation

$\mathcal{B}$EGINNING IN 1921, the New Brunswick Power Company started on a long range program of modernizing and improving its street railway. Up to this time, very little track renewal had been carried out, and most of the lines still had their original rails; in the centre of the city these dated back to 1894. Many of the cars were old, and the conversion to one-man had done nothing to improve their condition or appearance.

In 1922, the change in the "rule of the road" finally took place. In the Maritime provinces, as well as British Columbia, the rule had always been to drive on the left hand side, as in England, whereas the rest of North America drove on the right. With the increase of automobile traffic to and from the Maritimes this practice became inconvenient and dangerous, and so right hand driving was adopted. New Brunswick changed over on December 1st 1922, followed by Nova Scotia the following April 15th. By November 30th 1922, the company had completed changing its cars; it then posted instructions for passengers to get on and off the opposite side, and the change was made smoothly with little trouble.

About this time another dispute arose with the city regarding the distribution of electric power. During this controversy the company offered to sell out to the city, but the offer was declined. Eventually, in April 1923, the Federal Light and Traction Company of New York, which already controlled several traction companies in the US, bought a majority interest in the New Brunswick Power Company's securities, and so assumed control. The new management determined to continue the rehabilitation of the street railway, and in the next few years spent large sums of money on this project. The track rebuilding program was speeded up, and every year extensive renewals took place. In most cases, 82 lb. "T" rail was used, and the work was carried out in relatively small sections to minimize the time that any one line would be blocked. In some cases steel ties were laid, but these were too expensive for general use, and were confined to the busiest sections. During the next eight years, almost the entire track system was rebuilt, so by 1930 there was scarcely any street car track in Saint John more than ten years old.

Concurrently with the track renewal program, the rehabilitation of the rolling stock was undertaken. This was a more complicated situation due to the variety of equipment. In 1922 the company was considering the purchase of ten new cars, and plans were made to order these from a builder in Europe, but the price quoted was too high and the deal fell through. By 1923, the Birney Safety Car was in use on a large number of street railways of comparable size, and very serious consideration was given to equipping the entire system with Birneys, either new or second-hand. A great deal of discussion took place about the merits of air brakes versus hand brakes, especially the safety factor. The company continued to defend its policy of using hand brakes exclusively, maintaining that they were more positive in action, with fewer parts to get out of order, an important factor considering the steep hills involved. At any rate, the hand brakes carried the day, and remained in use until 1948.

Early in 1924, the company decided to rebuild its newer cars in its Wentworth Street shops, and then gradually replace older cars with new ones which it would also build itself, the idea of purchasing new cars having been given up. Under the direction of master mechanic Robert Harris, this remodelling was carried out starting in 1924. Twenty-four cars were rebuilt, including the last six open cars, which were converted to closed cars. The even-numbered 80 series of 1912 as well as the "Tillsonburg cars" of 1914 were also rebuilt. All cars were steel-sheathed

—Fred V. Stephens.

between the bulkheads; on the "Tillsonburg cars" this sheathing was flat, but on the older cars, formerly curve-sided, it sloped slightly inwards below the belt rail. Only one door on each side was provided, this being at the front, and serving as both entrance and exit in the same manner as on Birney cars. The rattan cross seats were replaced by longitudinal wooden seats which were less comfortable but did allow more standees. Galvanized iron vestibule-and bulkhead stanchions replaced the old bulkheads with sliding doors in an effort to speed up loading and unloading. Numerous other im-

provements were made, and to complete the "new look" a new paint scheme was adopted, the cars now being painted Brunswick green with cream trim, dark mahogany window frames and doors, with buff roofs, aluminum window guards, and black underbody. The first rebuilt car was placed in service November 11th 1924, and was followed by others over the next few months. Following this rebuilding, in 1925, two new cars were built, using some parts salvaged from older equipment. The new cars were numbered 130 and 132, and were 31 feet long, 7'10" wide, 11'6" high; had 20 foot bodies,

—Fred V. Stephens.

and seated 30 persons. They were mounted on Brill trucks, were powered by Westinghouse 101-B motors, and went into service late in 1925 and early 1926 respectively.

By this time, the old car barn on Main Street was little used except for the storage of old equipment, practically all the operation being from Wentworth Street and the west side car barn. By 1925, most of the old equipment had been scrapped, and in that year the old building, which dated back to the horse car days, was demolished. A skating rink was built on the site

Left:

A New Brunswick Power Company advertisement of the 1930s, showing car No. 142 and a list of routes. No. 142 was the last car to operate, in 1948.
                                    —Collection of the author.

Opposite, upper:

A high snow bank dwarfs car No. 150 on Manawagonish Road in 1934. Not a house nor an automobile is in sight.
                                    —New Brunswick Museum.

Opposite, lower:

A winterscape on Douglas Avenue about 1943. A snow plow and two street cars are snowbound, waiting for shovel crews to dig out the drift on the track.
                                    —Collection of R.D. Thomas.

and remained until 1967, when it burned, leaving the land vacant. Just in front of this site, in 1970, a few curved sections of rail were the last remnants of street car track still visible in Saint John, although unused for nearly fifty years.

In 1924, the Fairville line had been extended along the Manawagonish Road one-third of a mile to Moore's Hill, and in 1929 the Fairville and East Saint John lines were consolidated into a through service. At the East Saint John end, the city felt that the company was obligated, under an agreement made in 1914, to extend its line to the brickyard on the Red Head road. The company maintained that this service would not pay, but on December 2nd 1925, began an experimental shuttle service using a seven-passenger automobile running half a mile from the drydock to the brickyard. After two months and a loss of $1,000 the service was discontinued due to lack of passengers. A fine of $500 was imposed by the New Brunswick Public Utilities Commission, for failure to operate this run, but the company appealed, and there is no record that the fine was ever paid. However, this was the New Brunswick Power Company's first experiment with what might be termed a bus service, and was a forecast of things to come. In 1927, a 20-passenger Studebaker bus was purchased for sightseeing, but it was also used in shuttle service when car lines were interrupted during track rebuilding. 1927 was also the first year in which automobile competition became really noticeable. The winter that year was mild, and many autos were used through the winter, instead of being laid up as before. This started a habit not easily broken, even in bad weather, and the street car revenues suffered accordingly.

By 1927 it was apparent that the dark green paint job was not altogether satisfactory for the street cars, as the cars were not very visible, especially at night and in the thick fogs that periodically roll in from the Bay of Fundy. Therefore, a new colour scheme was adopted using Persian scarlet enamel with Pullman cream trim. Sash and doors were cherry red, roof slate colour, and trucks and miscellaneous fittings black. A new lacquer system of painting required only 7 days, compared to 10 days with the previous system. This contrasted markedly with the old method, in use before 1917, involving striping, varnishing, and detailed preparation. This old method had required 21 days, and produced a beautiful, long lasting finish, but was no longer justified economically, since the new paint job could be done at a cost of only $68.34 per car.

At this time, a salt car and a work car were built, and, in 1928, four more passenger cars joined the fleet. These were similar to those built in 1925-26 except that they had leather-covered cross seats which were much more comfortable than the wooden seats. They were built during spare time, so took nearly a year to complete, but they went into service late in 1928. The next year, four similar trams were built. They were placed in service by the beginning of 1930, and were the last cars acquired by the company. In 1930, the Fairville line was extended half a mile to Manchester's Corner, as originally planned, so completing the expansion of the street railway. The company intended to build more lines on the west side when the proposed new harbour bridge was opened, but the bridge was not built until the 1960s, twenty years after the street cars had gone, and no further car lines were ever constructed.

By 1930, the rehabilitation of the car lines was complete. The last of the older cars had been scrapped, reducing the total from 46 in 1927 to 34 in 1930. The former open cars, which had been rebuilt to closed configuration, were renumbered 150-160, even numbers, so producing a complete even-numbered series of 28 cars numbered from 106 to 160. In addition, cars 80 to 90, even numbers, completed the passenger car roster. The company's policy was to give the maximum service at the minimum cost, and, despite a high ticket cost of 8⅓¢, the average fare was only 5.5¢ due to the widespread use of the weekly pass scheme. Under the able direc-

tion of master mechanic Harris, the system had become self sufficient, and had even developed innovations copied by other companies. These included such widely divergent items as newspaper boxes on the cars, and a simple car body hoist for the shops. In 1930, the Wentworth car barn won an award for tasteful decoration and tidiness, and was considered to be "an object of civic pride". The improvements of the 1920s proved fortunate since they enabled the street railway system to survive the depression years of the Thirties and the war years of the Forties, and outlive many other systems of comparable size.

Photo above:

An official photograph of car No. 144 taken just after the car was completed in 1929. This class was the last lot of trams built for Saint John.
     —New Brunswick Hydroelectric Power Commission.

Photo below:

A popular children's make-believe streetcar game in Saint John was called "Ding, ding! This car goes up King!". No. 136 in Haymarket Square on a wintry day in the early 1940s is about to follow suit by mounting the King Street hill.
     —Railway Negative Exchange.

—Author's collection.

—Railway Negative Exchange.

—Canadian Railway & Marine World, August 1929.

Upper photo:

A promotional view of the Wentworth car barn in 1930, with four new street cars and a tower truck lined up outside. Note the large model aeroplane on the roof.

Centre photo:

A rare view of a 150 class car crossing the CPR tracks just west of Union Station, photographed from the station platform on a cold, foggy day. The trolley pole is at a high angle as the wire is positioned to clear the railway tracks. Note also the New Brunswick Power Company bus following the tram.

Photo right:

Another New Brunswick Power Company innovation was the provision of boxes for the sale of newspapers on the cars. This photograph also shows the platform arrangement used on all Saint John cars between 1924 and 1948.

57

10

Depression, Decline and War

*B*Y MID-1930 it was obvious that a state of deep depression had come, and that recovery would be slow and take many years. Street railway systems were hard hit, and it is in this period many lines, especially in smaller cities, either closed down completely, or were replaced by busses. In Saint John, the effect was not so drastic at first, although the number of passengers, which had reached more than 7,000,000 in 1929, gradually fell off to 4,600,000 by 1933. At this time, the Federal Government was undertaking major rebuilding of the harbour facilities on the west side, and this created some employment. However, this construction compelled the abandonment of some of the street car tracks and the west side car barn, which was replaced by a new barn at Tower and Ludlow streets in 1931. The depression was becoming worse, and in 1932 wage reductions of 10% to 20% came into effect, but even so, there was a loss of more than $40,000 that year. In 1934, further port development forced the removal of the track between Queen Square West and the harbour ferry. To take the place of the abandoned trackage, and to cover additional streets, the company began its first permanent bus service. At the same time, a new terminus of the line in Carleton was created by the building of a new track on Market Place. This was the last new track construction undertaken by the New Brunswick Power Company.

In April 1934, the forty-year exclusive franchise, granted to the Saint John Railway Company in 1894, expired, and, although the New Brunswick Power Company continued to operate, opinion was that this right was no longer exclusive. Nothing happened for two years, but in July 1936, the city council granted a bus franchise to F.C. Manning of Halifax, representing the Maritime Transit Company. This company was soon incorporated, and began a competing bus service, at first charging no fare. The New Brunswick Power Company appealed to the courts, and, after a legal battle, an injunction was issued, prohibiting bus competition. This injunction was subsequently upheld, and a new city council confirmed the rights of the New Brunswick Power Company under the agreement of 1894. Soon after this, the company inaugurated two bus routes on the west side, connecting with the street car lines.

In 1937, a report recommended that the city buy the assets of the New Brunswick Power Company and convert the street railway to busses as soon as possible. In part, the report stated: "The days of street railways in cities of a size comparable to Saint John are definitely over, and they cannot be made to pay". At this time there was serious consideration of bus substitution, but by now the depression was lifting, and the situation was not as bad as before, so the cars kept running. However, in July 1938, the 2½-mile Glen Falls line from Rothesay Avenue to Glen Falls was abandoned due to road widening absorbing the right-of-way. Three new busses were purchased to provide replacement service. This reduced the route mileage to 14.3, and the track mileage to 20.63, but no reduction of rolling stock was made. Such was the situation of the street railway in Saint John when World War II broke out in September 1939, shelving, for the time being, any plans for further bus substitution.

Opposite page, upper:

The Reversing Falls bridges, showing a Tillsonburg car just after leaving the "S" curve at the west end of the highway bridge. The piers of the old suspension bridge are visible at the extreme right in this 1938 photograph.
—Canadian Pacific Corporate Archives.

Opposite, lower:

King Street in 1930, showing two home-built cars going up the hill. Note that traffic now keeps to the right, and there are no more horses. Compare this with photograph on page 30, taken 24 years earlier.
—Wilson Studio.

An inside view of car No. 80, taken about 1937, showing the long, wooden seats installed in 1924. The man standing with his back to the camera is Hazen McLean, superintendent of the street railway, who began his career as a motorman in 1893, and retired in 1948 when operation ceased.

—Collection of R.D. Thomas.

Opposite, upper:

Car No. 122 in a snow scene on Manawagonish Road in 1934. Here the line is single-track.

—New Brunswick Museum.

Below:

Motorman Joseph Needham in front of car No. 106, decorated for the royal visit of King George VI and Queen Elizabeth on July 1st 1939. Mr. Needham drove No. 142 on its last run on August 7th 1948.

—R.D. Thomas.

During the Second World War, the importance of the port of Saint John was even greater than in World War I, 25 years earlier. For the next six years, Canada's two major Atlantic ports, Halifax and Saint John, saw ships of all descriptions sail for overseas on wartime missions. The effect on the street railway took various forms. The most obvious was a great increase in the number of passengers carried, the totals reaching nearly 11,000,000 for the street cars and 5,000,000 for the busses in 1945. The other effect was that the shortage of manpower and materials, coupled with rising costs, maintenance on track and equipment reduced to the barest minimum, with results that became more and more apparent as time went on. In the early Forties, Saint John was expanding to the north, and demands were made for bus service; accordingly some new busses were bought in 1942. In 1942, Fred Manning, (who had tried unsuccessfully to run busses in 1936) representing United Services Corporation of Halifax, bought the transportation division of the New Brunswick Power Company, with the intention of gradually converting to all-bus operation, thus being able to run the busses which he had been prevented from doing in 1936. This brought forth a legal battle, since all public transit was, for the duration of the war, under the Canadian Transit Controller, which had not given permission for this sale. Accordingly, the street railway was conveyed back to the Power Company. However, in 1943, to protect his investment, Mr. Manning purchased controlling interest in the New Brunswick Power Company.

At this time, the number of passengers carried was so great that new vehicles were needed, and the Transit Controller allowed the company to purchase more busses. Since there were only 34 street cars on the system, it was decided to confine these to certain routes. After inspection, busses replaced street cars on the Haymarket Square route, and on some streets in the South End, early in 1943. This was intended to be an emergency wartime measure to conserve equipment, but, in practice, regular street car service was never again operated on those routes south of King Street, nor on the line between Main Street and Haymarket Square. While all these tracks continued to be usable until the end of rail operations, by 1944 they were considered to be abandoned except for those sections required to reach the carbarn on Wentworth Street. Therefore, by the end of 1943, only three routes were in use:

— KING, from King and Charlotte streets to Indiantown.
— WEST, from Union and Charlotte to Rodney and Market Square, West Saint John.
— EAST, the long six-mile route from Tilton's Corner to East Saint John, via King and Prince Edward Streets.

These three routes required eighteen cars in regular service and eight more as extras, the remaining eight being kept for spares in the event of unusual demand or to replace cars that

Market Square about 1940. Note the New Brunswick Power Company bus between the two street cars.
—Gorham Photographic Services.

Wartime ~~CENSORED~~ Photos

During World War II, unauthorized photography of all means of transportation in the port city of Saint John was strictly forbidden. This included the street cars, though it is difficult to imagine what use enemy agents would have made of photographs of Saint John's then-ancient trams! However, the loyalties of the late Robert R. Brown, an eminent Canadian transportation historian and a frequent visitor to the Royal Hotel, were not to be questioned; a friendly and sympathetic management and staff provided him with discreet cover to avoid the prohibition, sometimes behind potted palms in the lobby, and on other occasions in strategically selected rooms. In this way, shooting between a lowered window blind (on top) and the window sill (bottom), Mr. Brown captured this unique record of wartime tram operation on King Street about 1942. The cars depicted are: Nos. 86, 158, 122, 160 top to bottom left, and 142, above.
—Late Robert R. Brown; Collection of R. Douglas Brown.

Right and centre, this page:

Two more views by the late Mr. Brown, this time from a second-floor, front room. Car No. 90 goes up the hill, while an unidentified 130 class car descends.
—Late Robert R. Brown; collection of R. Douglas Brown.

broke down in service. However, the trams performed a vital and essential service all through the dark days of World War II.

The company wanted to expand its bus lines, but had no exclusive bus franchise, and was unwilling to spend much money modernizing without this right. It sought to settle the matter, but another company, SMT (Eastern) a New Brunswick Corporation which already ran long distance busses, was interested in city bus operation. The latter company claimed that the power company had no right to operate busses at all, but did so only on sufferance, since the acts giving rights to the street railway mentioned only street cars. A final decision was deferred until after the war but the trend was to busses, and no matter which side won out it was obvious the trams would go. The deferred or totally-absent maintenance for several years had taken their toll on cars and track. The cars were uncomfortable and the jolting and swaying were incredible as they made their way over the rough and deteriorating rails. Of course it was a

vicious circle; the worse the condition of the track, the more jolting — and the more jolting, the faster the cars and track deteriorated. As World War II drew into its final phases in 1945, and the old cars struggled under an annual load of 11,000,000 passengers (almost equal to the whole population of Canada at that time) anyone could see that the end of the street cars in Saint John was very near. It was only a matter of time.

Above:

A 106 class car stopped in West Saint John about 1940, as a passenger boards.

—Collection of the author.

Below:

Car No. 90, on the Haymarket Square route, is about to climb King Street on the same day as the previous*photograph but almost two hours later. The "H" route, as well as Prince William Street (track in foreground), were converted to bus operation early in 1943.

*See lower photograph, page 56.

—Railway Negative Exchange.

11

End of the Trams

$\mathcal{T}$HE END OF the war found the street railway system in a sorry condition, worse than at almost any time in its history. The whole transportation system had been strained to the limit, breakdowns became more and more frequent, and much of the equipment was in poor condition. To put it simply, the street railway was worn out. The company had bought a number of busses to augment and replace street cars, as well as to add extra routes, and was clearly desirous of replacing the whole street car system with either busses or trolleybusses. But it was unwilling to embark on wholesale bus purchases until the question of the exclusive bus franchise was settled, and this was a question open to several interpretations.

The thirty-four cars had all remained in service throughout the war, but in 1945, car No. 82 was retired and used for spare parts, and another followed soon after. In July 1945, a six-year agreement was reached between company and the city and county of Saint John for the purchase of new, modern busses, the construction of a trolleybus system, and the gradual phasing out of all street cars over the next few years. However, this was opposed by SMT which immediately applied for an injunction holding up this agreement, charging it to be illegal since the New Brunswick Power Company had no clear licence to run busses. After much discussion, the injunction was dismissed on November 2nd on the grounds that the agreement did not cause damage to the taxpayers or the plaintiffs. Therefore, the agreement came into effect in November 1945, and the company proceeded with its bus plans.

During the next two and a half years the New Brunswick Power Company purchased a number of new busses, and the older trams were gradually retired and placed in dead storage. It is in this period that the 80 and 150 class cars and some of the 106 series trams made their last runs. The 32 cars in service in 1945 dwindled to only 9 — mostly of the 130 class — by 1948. This was enough to provide base service on the remaining lines, but in rush hours, even these lines were augmented by busses. On December 31st 1947, the provincially owned New Brunswick Hydro Corporation expropriated the power system of the New Brunswick Power Company,

leaving the latter with only the transportation and the gas system. Even so, there were many who felt the modernization program was not proceeding fast enough, and the city claimed the company ignored its pleas to speed up the conversion. The company claimed it was about ready to order trolleybusses, but it had suffered a setback as the result of a fire, early in 1948, which had destroyed several busses and one street car in the Wentworth barn. Also, SMT was still hopeful of obtaining the bus franchise for Saint John in place of the power company, and they had strong support in city council and elsewhere.

Matters came to a head on February 12th 1948, when the city council passed a resolution to the effect that the trams were hopelessly antiquated and inadequate, and petitioning the Provincial Legislature to cancel all transportation rights of the New Brunswick Power Company. The bill was introduced in the Legislature in April, and was the subject of much heated debate for several days. The city claimed that the company had not lived up to its part of the 1945 agreement, that the "1914 vintage street cars" were "a menace to public safety" and "a laughing stock to Canada". Moreover, the streets were in poor condition adjacent to the tracks, and the city was unwilling to pave them until the tracks were taken up. It was also stated that the street cars were involved in 160 accidents from 1945 to 1947, due largely to the 45% increase in automobile traffic in that period. In vain the company argued that it was modernizing as fast as it could, but equipment was hard to get in the immediate post war period. Public sentiment was against the New Brunswick Power Company, and, although it put up a good fight, it was doomed to failure.

The bill passed on April 23rd, and the city was given permission to cancel all transportation rights granted to the New Brunswick Power Company and its predecessors, as far back as 1866, on seventy-five days notice. As a consolation, the city was to assume the whole cost of removing the rails and re-paving the streets. It was unfortunate that the cancellation of the transportation rights caused considerable hard feeling among some of the long-time employees of the New Brunswick Power Company.

During the December 1947 storm, the crew of sweeper No. 4 could afford only a few moments' pause at the West Saint John terminus before heading back to the city to continue the battle against the steadily-falling snow.

—Fred V. Stephens.

Below:

A King tram going up the street of that name on June 28th 1947.

—Anthony Clegg.

Opposite page, upper and centre:

Two views of cars crossing the CPR tracks by Union Station on June 28th 1947. The trainshed was demolished about 1960, and the station building in 1973.

Opposite page, lower:

Car No. 146 on Charlotte Street on June 28th 1947 passing the historic city market, built in 1876, and still in use after more than a century.

—Anthony Clegg, both photos.

—Anthony Clegg.

Car No. 112 descends the steep hill on Pitt Street, coming off duty and returning to the barn, on June 28th 1947.
—Anthony Clegg.

Below:

A general view of seven of the stored cars, on June 28th 1947.
—Anthony Clegg.

Opposite page, lower:

Sweeper No. 3 busily at work, passing through Haymarket Square during the great storm of December 26th 1947. This storm, one of the worst on the Atlantic coast in a century, was the climax of the career of the sweepers. In a few more months, the street car system would be a thing of the past.
—Fred V. Stephens.

Shortly thereafter, the city served notice that all transportation rights of the New Brunswick Power Company would cease at midnight on August 7th, 1948 and, to the surprise of almost no one, concluded an agreement with SMT for the latter to operate busses. On June 14th, a franchise was granted to SMT which immediately formed a subsidiary, City Transit Limited, to operate the busses. The franchise came into effect on July 1st, and on that day, City Transit placed 36 new busses in service. The busses had just been delivered, and there was no time to give them a final paint job, so they started operating in an undercoat paint colour of dark gray, with very small white numbers. The New Brunswick Power Company made one last fight and advertised for 75 bus drivers and 12 street car operators. For a while both companies ran rival services on the same routes, and it is a wonder that no one was killed as busses of the two organizations raced each other to pick up passengers. Gradually, however, the power company realized that the contest was hopeless, and reduced its service over the next month. The city was anxious to start tearing up the tracks, but the company was prepared to fight to the bitter end, and continued to run one street car, No. 142, on three or four trips a day over the whole system, just to hold its right. Starting early in 1948, even before the cancellation of the franchise, the older cars, retired between 1945 and 1947, were taken out of storage, dismantled at Wentworth car barns, and the bodies sold to individuals. During June and July 1948, the newer cars also disappeared one by one, and nearly all were gone by the time the franchise expired. By the end of July, all the power company's busses were out of service, and many were sold to other cities for further use. The last remnant of the company's transportation service was old No. 142 which continued to run back and forth, like a ghost from the past, carrying few, if any, passengers, until the expiry of the franchise.

City Transit Limited, a subsidiary of SMT (Eastern) Limited — New Brunswick's interurban bus carrier — began regular city bus service on July 1st 1948. This announcement appeared in newspapers at that time.
—Public Archives of Canada, L5217.

In an apparent final gesture of defiance at the new City Transit Limited, the New Brunswick Power Company, on July 1st 1948, advertised for 75 bus drivers and 12 street car operators.
—Public Archives of Canada, L5218.

Saturday, August 7th 1948, car 142 made its customary runs, and that evening set out from the car barn for its last trip. On hand were Hazen McLean, the superintendent, who had been with the company and its predecessors since the start of electrification, Joseph Needham, the operator assigned to that run, and operators Frank Quigley, Roy Stephens, Arthur Cummings, and Carl Conrad. Also present was Mr. Sutherland of Halifax, representing the owners, but there were no passengers and no reporters. The last to board was operator Cecil Joyce who ran a grocery store on Main Street, and the car waited outside while he closed the store and got aboard. On this last run, all present took turns running the car for a short distance. As No. 142 headed east along Main Street for the last time, there were still people living who could remember that Good Friday fifty-five years before when the first trial run with electric power had been made. There were even those who could still vaguely recall the days of the horse cars, stretching back to the long-gone People's Street Railway, and all the trials and tribulations of the various companies down through the years. The street cars had served Saint John long and well, but now their day was over. No. 142 headed back east through the dark, almost-deserted streets, clattering over the familiar old tracks to King Square, then turned towards Wentworth St. There was no fanfare, celebration, or public mourning as the car arrived back at the car barn just before midnight. No. 142 was put into the barn, the trolley was pulled down off the wire, and the tram era in New Brunswick was over.

Above:

This controller handle was used on the last run of car No. 142 on August 7th 1948. With it, the street car era in Saint John was concluded.
—Author.

Opposite page, upper:

No. 122 going up Princess Street near Sydney Street. This photograph was taken on June 28th 1947 after regular service on this line had been discontinued. The car is returning to the barns after the morning rush hour.
—Anthony Clegg.

Opposite page, centre:

In 1949, the body of car No. 86 was photographed in a field on Loch Lomond Road; it was destroyed within two years.
—R.D. Thomas.

Opposite page, lower:

The storage yard again, in June 1948, with the sweepers being stripped. In the background, the brushes from sweepers 1 and 2 are burning, while in the foreground No. 3 is already stripped. Note the car supports (see photo page 53) on the ground in front of No. 3.
—Author.

12

Conclusion

$\mathcal{T}$HIRTY YEARS have passed since the last street car ran in Saint John. A whole new generation has grown up since then, and the memories of the little red cars are fast fading into the past. Physical traces of the system are few and far between. As early as August 9th 1948, crews were at work uprooting the rails and now, the only place where track can still be seen in the 1970s is in front of the site of the old Main Street car barn, abandoned in 1925, where two 20-foot sections, complete with paving stones, are still visible after more than fifty years of disuse. The power house still stands at the corner of Dock and Union streets, but the one-fifth size model of a street car that once graced its front corner window is gone, and is now in the New Brunswick Museum. The car barn and shops on Wentworth Street also still remain, but have been converted to other uses. The car bodies that were sold and which dotted the countryside for years, have gradually disappeared. Nine of them are together and used as storehouses, and a few others, mostly in the last stages of decay, can still be seen. Only one has been historically preserved. Car No. 82 was rescued in 1962 and sent to the Canadian Railway Museum at Delson, Quebec. This car, which is the only example of a street car from the Maritimes to come to a museum, had extensive restoration work done on it in 1971 and 1972, so that the car body appears as it did in the 1930s. Other relics and information, once easy of access, have been scattered far and wide, and much has been irretrievably lost.

City Transit Limited still operates the bus service in Saint John, and has modernized and upgraded its fleet over the years. For more than two decades it was able to maintain excellent service with moderate fares compared to many other cities. In recent years, however, increasing expenses and reduced patronage, due no doubt to automobile competition, have forced the company to implement higher fares and considerable reduction of service especially on weekends. Although those who criticized the operation of Sunday street cars in 1887 might be happy with the curtailment of Sunday service, those of their descendants who must use public transport are inconvenienced today. Whether Saint John's transit system will continue under a private company or pass to public ownership is a pressing question which will likely be decided in the near future. However, the maintenance of good, dependable public transportation is as important to a city today as it was in the days of the street cars. The question as to whether the right steps were taken in 1948 will probably never be answered, but it is significant that Halifax, which adopted trolley busses in 1949, has since converted entirely to diesel busses. One can only speculate if Saint John would have done likewise eventually, even if trolley busses had replaced the trams.

Much of the dislike vented on the street cars in their last years has faded with the passage of time. These days, when more and more attention is being turned to relics of the past, it is realized that the trams played an important part in the history of Saint John. True, they were not as impressive or romantic as the sailing ships that once sailed into the harbour from all over the world, nor the wood-burning steam locomotives of the pioneer railways, but they are just as extinct, and each of these means of transportation played its role and played it well. Today, in the mad rush of traffic, and the overpowering fumes from cars, trucks and busses, many people must secretly mourn the passing of the trolley era, and perhaps on some dark, foggy night, when the ghosts are about at the foot of King Street, one may almost expect to see a little red street car come out of the fog, and carry one back, in imagination, to those pre-pollution days when electric cars were the chief means of public transportation in the Loyalist City.

Photo above:

Car No. 128 leaves Wentworth barn on a float in June 1948.

—Wilson Studio.

Photo below:

The crew of New Brunswick Power Company's line truck at work taking down the trolley wire on Britain Street on August 14th 1948, following the termination of service.
—Fred V. Stephens; Stephens Collection;
National Museum of Science and Technology.

Acquisitions, Disposals
and Total Cars

Year	Cars Acquired			Cars Disposed of			Cars at End of Year		
	CLOSED	OPEN	TOTAL	CLOSED	OPEN	TOTAL	CLOSED	OPEN	TOTAL
1887	10.	0.	10.	0.	0.	0.	10.	0.	10.
1888	4.	0.	4.	0.	0.	0.	14.	0.	14.
1892	6.	0.	6.	0.	0.	0.	20.	0.	20.
1893	6.	0.	6.	14.	0.	14.	12.	0.	12.
1894	9.	3.	12.	9.	0.	9.	12.	3.	15.
1895	2.	0.	2.	0.	0.	0.	14.	3.	17.
1898	4.	5.	9.	3.	0.	3.	15.	8.	23.
1903	7.	0.	7.	1.	0.	1.	21.	8.	29.
1904	0.	6.	6.	0.	0.	0.	21.	14.	35.
1905	0.	7.	7.	0.	0.	0.	21.	21.	42.
1906	8.	1.	9.	0.	0.	0.	29.	22.	51.
1907	0.	7.	7.	0.	0.	0.	29.	29.	58.
1908	4.	0.	4.	6.	0.	6.	27.	29.	56.
1910	0.	0.	0.	2.	3.	5.	25.	26.	51.
1912	6.	0.	6.	0.	0.	0.	31.	26.	57.
1913	7.	0.	7.	0.	0.	0.	38.	26.	64.
1914	12.	0.	12.	4.	0.	4.	46.	26.	72.
1919	0.	0.	0.	0.	0.	0.	46.	26.	72.
1920	0.	0.	0.	3.	12.	15.	43.	14.	57.
1921	0.	0.	0.	10.	8.	18.	33.	6.	39.
1925	2.	0.	2.	0.	0.	0.	35.	6.	41.
1927	6.	0.	6.	0.	6.	6.	41.	0.	41.
1928	4.	0.	4.	3.	0.	3.	42.	0.	42.
1929	4.	0.	4.	7.	0.	7.	39.	0.	39.
1930	0.	0.	0.	5.	0.	5.	34.	0.	34.
1948	0.	0.	0.	34.	0.	34.	0.	0.	0.
TOTAL	101.	29.	130.	101.	29.	130.	na	na	na

Opposite page, upper:

Car No. 82 disembarking three passengers at Haymarket Square in 1942. This is the only known photograph in service of the only Saint John street car to be officially preserved.

—Collection of Peter Cox.

Opposite page, centre:

No. 82 was destined for eventual preservation, but not before it had undergone much deterioration. In this photograph, taken in July 1948, No. 82 (left) and No. 154 (right) are in the yard of an abandoned farmhouse on Golden Grove Road. The fate of No. 154 is unknown, but No. 82 had several more moves ahead of it.

—Author.

Opposite page, lower:

Fourteen years later and much the worse for wear, No. 82's body is securely strapped down to a CPR flat car in Saint John in December 1962, ready for the 500-mile trip to the Canadian Railway Museum, then under construction at Delson, Quebec.

—Author's Collection.

Photo above:

Eventually, after many delays, restoration work was undertaken on No. 82. Here it rests on a contemporary truck outside one of the display buildings at the Canadian Railway Museum. When restoration is complete, the car body will be about 8 inches lower on the truck frame.

—Author.

Below: Two Tillsonburg-built cars were joined together to form a house.

—R.D. Thomas.

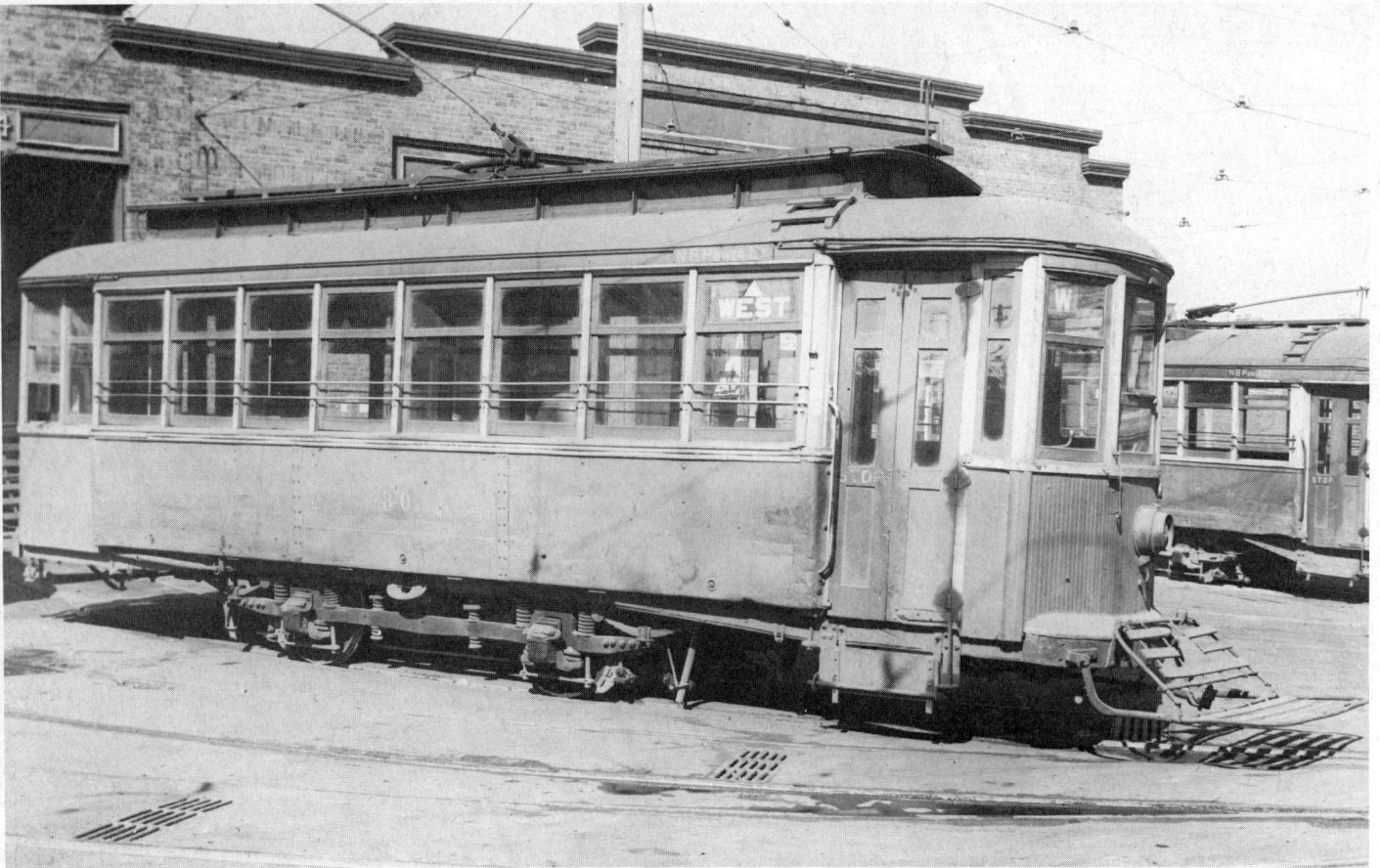

—M.D. McCarter.

Car No. 80, the first of its class, posed outside Wentworth car barn on May 20th 1946. This car would be in service only a few weeks more.

Tillsonburg-built No. 122 at Wentworth barn on May 20th 1946. Notice the many dents in the car side, evidence of the hazards of increasing traffic.

—M.D. McCarter.

Home-built snow plow No. 7 was specially posed at Wentworth barn on Monday, May 20th 1946. The folding wings could clear a wide swath on either side of the track.
—M.D. McCarter.

Ⅱ: ROSTER of WORK CARS

All are electric unless noted

Car Numbers	How Many	Kind of Car	Length Between Bulkheads (in Feet)	Type of Roof	Year Acquired	Acquired From	Remarks	Year(s) of Disposal	Details of Disposal
?	2	Horse Drawn Snow Plows	?	?	1887	Harris and Co.	Used in Horse car period and early electric days.	C.1895	Scrapped.
?	1	Flanger	?	?	1893	Consolidated Electric Co.	In service Dec. 12, 1893. Otherwise unknown.	C.1895	Scrapped.
?	2	Sweepers		Arch	1894	Ottawa Car Co. (Ahearn and Soper)		C.1924	Scrapped.
?	2	Snow Plows		?	1902	?		C.1926	Scrapped.
?	1	Sweeper		?	1906	?		C.1928	Scrapped.
?	1	Snow Plow		?	1907	?		C.1926	Scrapped.
?	1	Sweeper		?	1907	?		C.1928	Scrapped.
1, 2	2	Sweepers		Flat Arch	1924	McGuire Cummings		1948	Bodies sold. Trucks scrapped.
3, 4	2	Sweepers		Flat Arch	1928	Probably McGuire Cummings		1948	Bodies sold. Trucks scrapped.
5, 6, 7	3	Combination Snow Plow and Work Car.		Arch	1926	New Brunswick Power Co.	Used trucks from old cars.	1948	Bodies sold. Trucks scrapped.
8	1	Hauling Car		None	1927	New Brunswick Power Co.	Used truck from old car.	C.1940	Scrapped.
25	1	Stores Car	12	Bombay	C.1895	Saint John Railway Co.	Ex. Passenger Car 25. Ex. 1887-88 Horse car.	C.1928	Scrapped.
81	1	Welding Car	21	Deck	C.1921	New Brunswick Power Co.	Rebuilt from open car 81 built 1907.	Before 1940	Scrapped.
100	1	Stores Car (Trailer)	20	Deck	C.1928	New Brunswick Power Co.	Ex. Passenger car 100 with motors removed. Ex. Buffalo car, built 1903.	C.1940	Scrapped.

—R.S. Melvin, both photos.

II: ROSTER of PASSENGER CARS

All are single-truck, double-end electric cars unless indicated

Car Numbers	How Many	Kind of Car	Length Between Bulkheads (in Feet)	Type of Roof	Year Acquired	Acquired From	Remarks	Year(s) of Disposal	Details of Disposal
1-10	10	Closed Horse Cars	12	Bombay	1887	M. Feigel Car Co. New Utrecht, N.Y.	Five windows per side. 8 cars in service in time for line's opening Oct. 17, 1887. Other 2 by year-end.	1893	8 Cars scrapped. 6 cars converted to electric cars and renumbered 21-26.
11-14	4	Closed Horse Cars	12	Bombay	1888	John Stephenson Co. New York, N.Y.	Six windows per side.	1893	
15-20	6	Single-end Closed cars	16	Bombay	1892	West End Street Railway Co. Boston, Mass.	First electric cars in Saint John. Ex. West End Street Ry. Horse Cars Nos. 115, 127, 147, 233, 235 239. Built before 1887, and used in East Boston and Chelsea. Purchased Sep. 1892, electrified, and placed in service in 1893.	1894 to 1899	Scrapped.
21-26	6	Single-end Closed cars	12	Bombay	1893	Consolidated Electric Co.	Rebuilt from 6 horse cars of 1-14 series and electrified.	1894 to 1899	No. 25 converted to work car. Others scrapped.
27-29	3	Open Cars		Deck	1894	Ottawa Car Co. (Ahearn and Soper)	First Open cars in Saint John.	C.1911	Scrapped
30-38	9	Closed cars with Vestibules	18	Deck	1894	Ottawa Car Co. (Ahearn and Soper)	First cars of Saint John Railway Co.	C.1910 to 1921	No. 37 destroyed c1900 Others scrapped.
39-40	2	Closed cars Same as 30-38	18	Deck	1895	Ottawa Car Co. (Ahearn and Soper)		C.1910 to 1921	Scrapped.
41, 43, 46, 47, 49.	5	Single-end Open cars	21	Flat Arch.	1898	Montreal Street Railway	Similar to Montreal open cars of 359 class.	C.1920	Scrapped.
42, 44, 45, 48.	4	Closed cars Similar to 30-40	18	Deck	1898	Ottawa Car Co. (Ahearn and Soper)		C.1921	Scrapped
Second 37	1	Closed Car	18	Deck	1900	Montreal Street Railway	Ex. MSR No. 240 built by Ottawa Car Co. (Ahearn and Soper) in 1893.	C.1920	Scrapped.
50-55	6	Double-truck Closed Cars		"Montreal"	1903	Montreal Street Railway	Ex. Montreal Park and Island Railway Co. Nos. 200-205, Built by MSR in 1900. Only double-truck cars ever to run in Saint John.	1908	Nos. 50-52 sold to Berlin, Ontario. Became Nos. 16, 18, 20. Nos. 53-55 sold to Levis, Quebec. Became Nos. 100, 101, 102.
56-61	6	Open Cars		Deck	1904	Ottawa Car Co.		C.1920	Scrapped.

Continued on opposite page . . .

Above:

The model of car No. 132 which was formerly displayed at the New Brunswick Power building. This model, which is six feet long, has since been restored and is preserved by the New Brunswick Museum.

—New Brunswick Museum.

Opposite, upper left:

The old headquarters building and power house of the New Brunswick Power Company still survives in Saint John. In this 1970 view, note the large corner display window where a model of car No. 132 was displayed for many years.

—Author.

Opposite, centre left:

A rare view of one of the 106 class trams under construction in the shops of the Tillsonburg Electric Car Company in Tillsonburg, Ontario, in 1914.

Opposite, upper right:

Work car No. 8, made from the truck of an old passenger car, photographed at Indiantown on August 29th 1940.

Opposite, centre right:

Work car trailer No. 100, ex-passenger car No. 100, photographed at Indiantown on August 29th 1940. This was the last of the 1903 Brill-built cars purchased from Buffalo, New York, in 1913.

Car Numbers	How Many	Kind of Car	Length Between Bulkheads (in Feet)	Type of Roof	Year Acquired	Acquired From	Remarks	Year(s) of Disposal	Details of Disposal
62-68	7	Open Cars		Deck	1905	Ottawa Car Co.		C.1920	Scrapped.
69-74	6	Closed Cars	18	Deck	1906	Ottawa Car Co.		C.1925 to 1929	Bodies scrapped. Trucks of some cars used on 130-class cars
75	1	Open Car	?	?	C.1906	Unknown (Probably second-hand)		C.1921	Scrapped.
76, 78	2	Closed Cars		Deck	1906	Ottawa Car Co.		C.1928 to 1929	Bodies scrapped. Trucks probably used on 130-class cars.
81-93 Odd Numbers	7	Open Cars	21	Deck	1907	Ottawa Car Co.	Last Open cars.	1921 to 1927	No.81 converted to Welding Car C.1921. 83 to 93 (Odd) rebuilt to closed cars in 1927 and renumbered 150 to 160 (even).
401,465 560,567	4	Closed Cars	20	Deck	1908	Boston Elevated Railway Co.	Rebuilt in 1893 by West End Street Ry. by enlarging, and electrifying, 16-foot Boston Horse Cars. Kept Boston numbers in Saint John.	C.1921	Scrapped.
80-90 Even Numbers	6	Closed Cars	21	Deck	1912	Ottawa Car Co.	First Saint John cars built for "Pay-as-you-enter" operation. Rebuilt by N.B. Power Co. in 1924-1925, with steel side sheathing.	1948	Bodies sold. Trucks scrapped. No. 82 preserved at Canadian Railway Museum.
92-104 Even Numbers	7	Closed Cars	20	Deck	1913	Buffalo, N.Y.	Ex. 1000-1049 series built by J.G. Brill Co. in 1903.	C.1928 to 1930	No. 100 converted to work car. Others scrapped. Some trucks used on newer cars.
106-128 Even Numbers	12	Closed Cars	20	"Turtle Back" Arch	1914	Tillsonburg Electric Car Co. Tillsonburg, Ontario	Rebuilt by N.B. Power Co. in 1924 to 1925, with steel side sheathing.	1948	Bodies sold. Trucks scrapped.
130-132 Even Numbers	2	Closed Cars	20	Arch	1925	New Brunswick Power Co.	Used trucks from old cars.	1948	Bodies sold. Trucks scrapped.
134-140 Even Numbers	4	Closed Cars	20	Arch	1928	New Brunswick Power Co.	Used trucks from old cars	1948	Bodies sold. Trucks scrapped.
142-148 Even Numbers	4	Closed Cars	20	Arch	1929	New Brunswick Power Co.	Used trucks from old cars. No. 142 was last car in service (Aug. 7 1948).	1948	Bodies sold. Trucks scrapped.
150-160 Even Numbers	6	Closed Cars	21	Deck	1927	New Brunswick Power Co.	Rebuilt from open cars. 83 to 93 (Odd) built by Ottawa Car Co. in 1907.	1948	Bodies sold. Trucks scrapped.

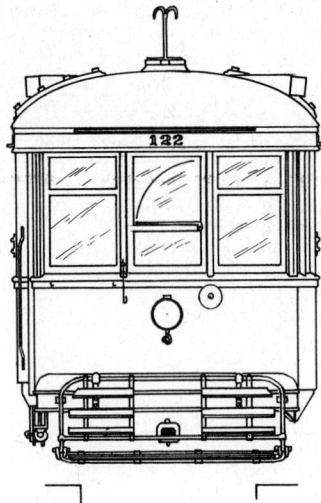
Car 122, end view.

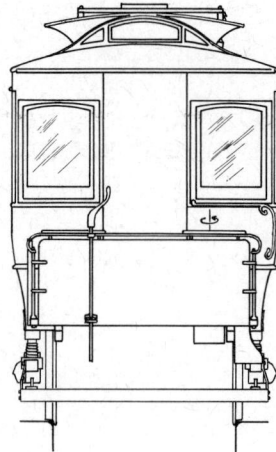
Car 21, end view.

Diagrams

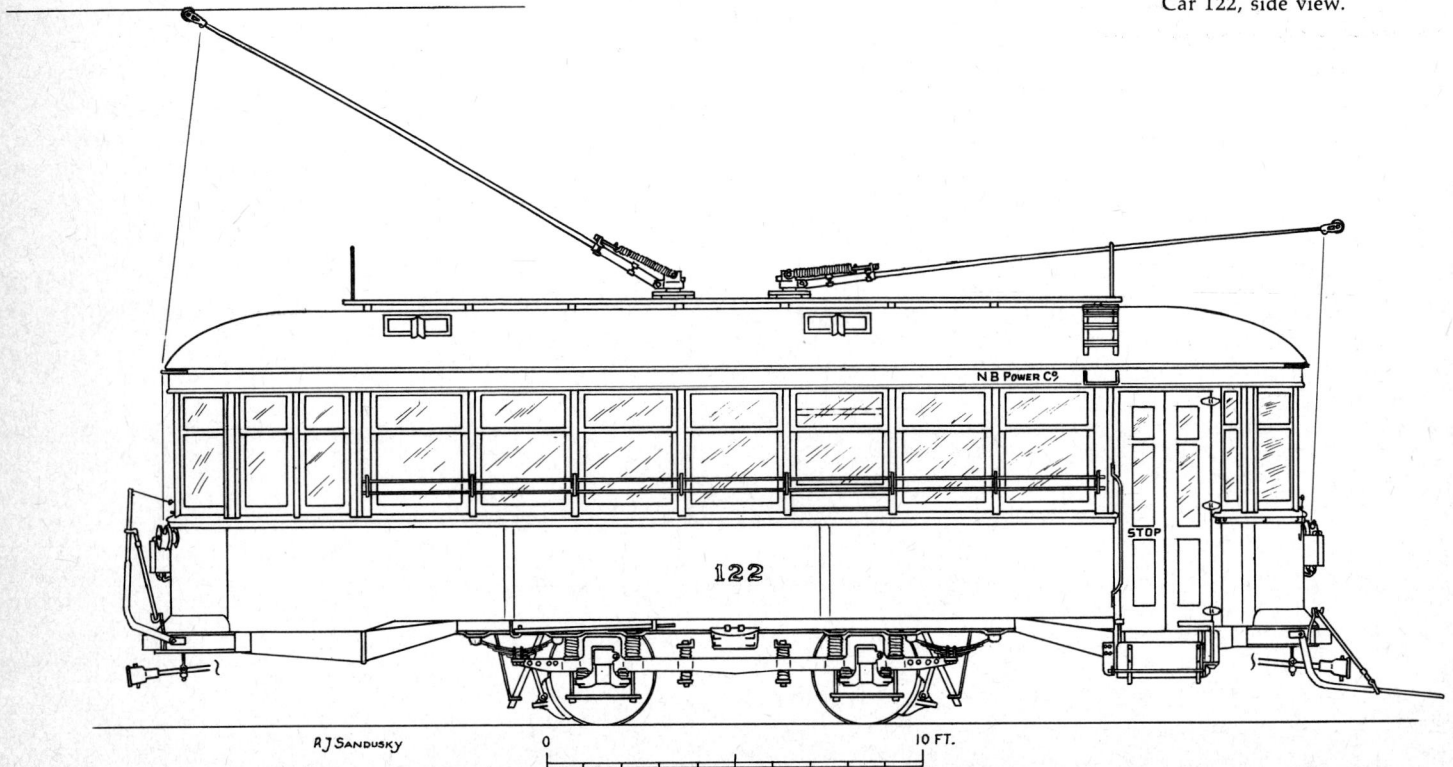
Car 122, side view.

R.J. Sandusky   0   10 FT.

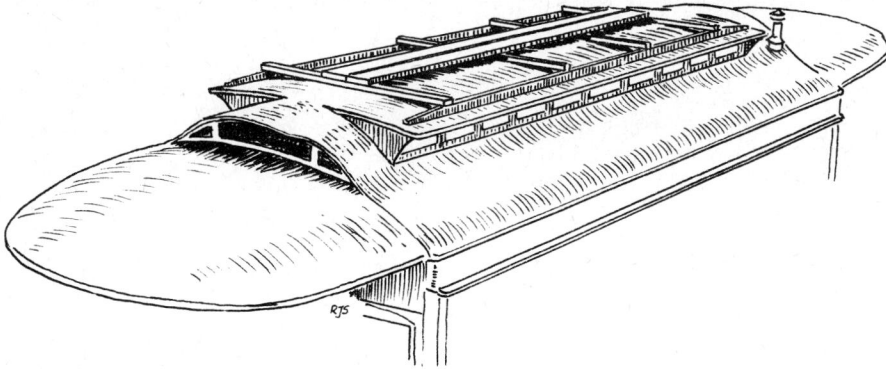

These diagrams were drawn by Robert Sandusky.

Two cars are shown: No. 21, and No. 122.

Electric car No. 21, as converted by Consolidated Electric Company in 1893 from a Saint John horsecar.

Car 122, a Tillsonburg-built car of the 106 class, as rebuilt by New Brunswick Power Company in 1925.

Also included is a diagram to illustrate the "Bombay Roof".

Car 21, side view.

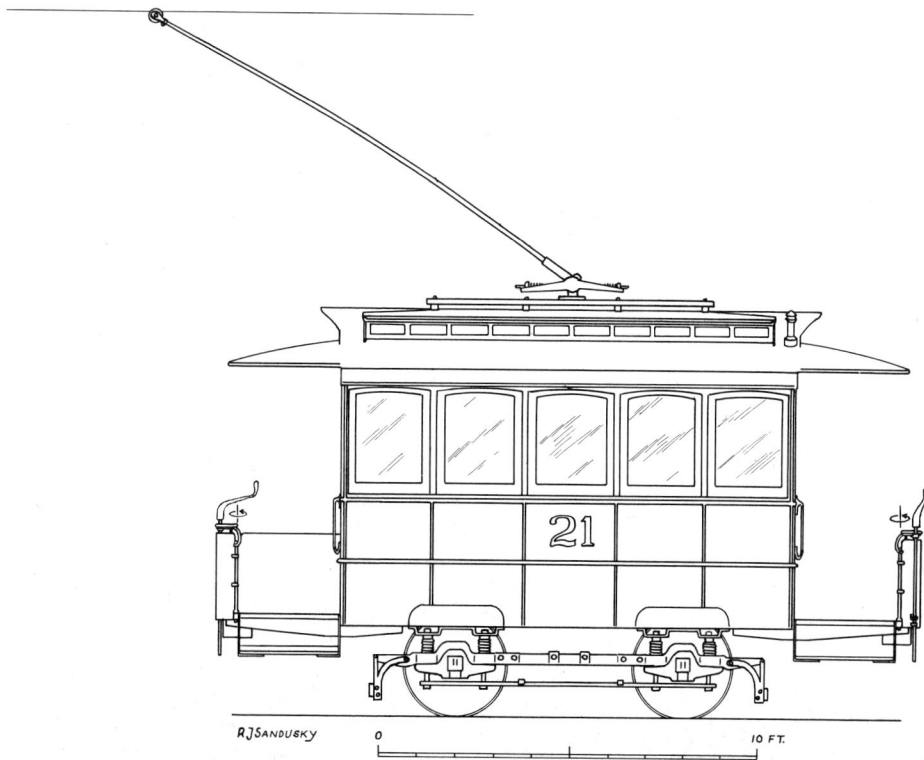

Car 156 on the curve leading to the yard beside Wentworth barn on a sunny Monday morning May 20th 1946. Although still in rush-hour service, No. 156 was near the end of the line.

—M.D. McCarter.

Car 148, the last car built for Saint John, seen at Wentworth car barn on May 20th 1946.

—M.D. McCarter.